A MODERN INTRODUCTION TO
MORAL PHILOSOPHY

A MODERN INTRODUCTION TO MORAL PHILOSOPHY

by

Alan Montefiore

LONDON

ROUTLEDGE & KEGAN PAUL

First published 1958
by Routledge & Kegan Paul Ltd
Broadway House, Carter Lane, E.C.4

Printed in Great Britain
by Compton Printing Limited
London and Aylesbury

Second impression 1964
Third impression 1967

PREFACE

THIS book would have been very much more obscure and more frequently mistaken than it is without the generous and patient help of four of my friends. My most grateful thanks are due to Miss Joy Coles and Miss Patricia Gleeson for their many warnings of passages which they, as non-philosophers, found hard or impossible to understand, and for their help in making these passages clearer; also to Professor D. J. O'Connor and Mr. R. F. Atkinson for their thorough-going criticisms and comments from a professional point of view. I am equally grateful to another friend, Mrs. Margaret Harvey, for having undertaken the tedious and difficult task of compiling the index.

I need hardly add that any obscurities and mistakes that remain are entirely my own responsibility.

ALAN MONTEFIORE.

Keele, May, 1958.

CONTENTS

1

INTRODUCTION

ACCORDING to its title this book is an introduction to moral philosophy. But it must be admitted straight away that as a title this is neither novel, inspiring nor informative. So before doing anything else I had better try and give some more exact indication of what kind of book it is intended to be. This should provide at least some sort of warning for those who very wisely prefer to read the first chapter of a book in the shop before deciding (usually) not to buy it after all.

The first and most important warning is that it is seriously intended to be an introduction. It is not, therefore, intended for those who are already philosophers, professional or otherwise; and I should make it clear at the outset that any interest that it may have for them will be almost entirely accidental.

The second warning is of almost the opposite sort. For though as an introduction this really is meant for people who do not know any philosophy to start with, it is still bound in places to demand a fairly concentrated attention. In one way, indeed, it would be something of a fraud if it did not. For it would be wrong to give the impression that philosophy is an entirely simple subject. This is not because it is a particularly technical one—though it may admittedly have its own (often exaggerated) technicalities. It is rather because it nearly always involves keeping in mind a great number of points at once, and the ability to follow a sustained and systematic argument, both of which things need a good deal of practice. So an introduction that was so determined to be clear that it succeeded only by giving no idea whatsoever of how complex the subject can be, could

1

not properly be considered as an introduction to philosophy at all.

Still, this warning should not be taken too grimly. It is true that the overall continuity of the argument will mean that skipping may very well lead to confusions. But, on the other hand, I have ended each chapter by trying to sum up its main points. And I have also tried as best I could at no stage to forget that I should not assume any knowledge of philosophy beyond what will have been given already in previous chapters.

There is one other warning to be issued: namely that the sort of philosophy to which this is an introduction is specifically the sort of philosophy that is at present generally practised in this country. There are two main reasons for this apparently parochial restriction. The first lies in the fact that British philosophy is for the most part so very different in style, assumption and method from most philosophy on the continent that it would be impossible to embark on them both at once; and it is after all British philosophy that is most likely to be the more immediately relevant and accessible to the ordinary British reader. Most people, of course, know nothing at all even about British philosophers. Of those that do know something, many know little more than that they are at the moment largely preoccupied with questions of language. It is often thought, too, that this preoccupation leads them to be generally intricate and obscure, and always futile and remote; and that with all their playing with definitions, the present-day philosophers have made their tower not even of real ivory, but rather of dry white bone from which the flesh has long since withered away.

Some philosophers, no doubt, do spend too much of their time in analysing other philosophers' analyses from towers such as these. But then at any time and in any school of philosophy there are obviously bound to be some who are better or worse, greater or lesser than others. At any rate, in trying to explain and to show something of what this modern British philosophy is like, I shall try also to show how its concern with language can in fact arise out of and involve issues which are entirely serious and anything but remote; how, for instance, our view of the basis of our own principles of value can turn on the answers we give to questions that may seem at first sight to be both technical and irrelevant. I have naturally tried to do this as clearly as I could. But I have also, I admit without apology, deliberately introduced a certain limited number of the commoner and more important terms of professional jargon. I have done this not only because jargon, if not allowed to run wild, can often be a most useful and even necessary device—shorter, more precise than the alternative expressions that may (or may not) be available in ordinary speech and, by reason of its very unfamiliarity, less liable to carry unwanted and misleading associations; but more especially because anyone who may perhaps be stimulated to grapple further with the questions raised in this book, will be helped to make his way about more advanced discussions if he has already met and used some of the commoner tools of the trade. This indeed has been my chief aim; not to provide definitive solutions, but to give to someone who has not done any philosophy before enough of the hang of it to be able to go on with the arguments for himself. For even though he may not himself want to become a philosopher, to have taken part in philosophic discussion is in the end the only effective way to appreciate what philosophy is about.

If, then, philosophy involves a certain sort of systematic discussion, the best way to see what sort of discussion this is, is to start to discuss. The whole of this book, therefore, will grow out of and around the consideration of one particular problem. This brings me to my second reason for sticking to the current British type of philosophy. It is quite simply that this is how philosophical problems most naturally present themselves to me. This in its turn is, of course, very largely due to the accident of where I was first taught to think about these things, at Oxford which is a notorious centre of what is known as linguistic analysis. It would obviously be absurd to pretend that there is nothing but confusion in all other types of philosophy or that this method avoids all really serious difficulties. But it does, I think, provide the best way in which at any rate to start. For it can hardly be seriously denied that whatever else one may wish to discuss, one must at all times try to keep clear the meaning of what is being said; or at the very least, if this is sometimes impossible, to be as clear as one can be about where ambiguities must for the time being remain and the reasons why they must do so. And this is one of the most characteristic interests of modern British philosophy. For it is essentially concerned with problems of meaning; not, I should add, of the sort that can be settled by a hasty definition or two, but the less obvious, far more tricky, far more dangerous kind that are often unnoticed as problems at all but which, once they are looked into, lead on to other problems and to others and to others.

So I shall start out from one particular problem, trying to sketch in by the way just enough of the background to show how it has come to seem natural to tackle the problem from this angle. In doing this I must confess to having made only an occasional attempt to sort out the sources of the various views I put forward. For the most part I would anyhow find it very hard to do so. So much of what is said here has been floating around in the philosophical air that it is not easy to tell in exactly which part of the air one has absorbed what. But in any case in a discussion which is new to the reader in the way that this one must be, continual references to names and journals of which he has never heard would tend to provide little but distraction and irritation. So I must apologise most humbly in advance to all those whose views may be mentioned, but whose names may not.

It follows from this that any small claims to originality on my part would be both dubious and irrelevant. It is, however, only right to say that I should expect a good many philosophers to disagree with some of the arguments that

4

I use, particularly towards the second part of the book. Still, I do not think that this matters very much; (indeed it is hardly avoidable in view of the ways in which philosophers all tend to disagree among themselves). This is not after all intended to be any sort of a survey, but an introduction to philosophy by way of a philosophical discussion; and the reader should be encouraged rather than anything else by the thought that if and when he disagrees with my views on the problems discussed, he has a very reasonable chance of finding himself in the most respectable philosophic company. Of course, I have tried not to make mistakes—though since one cannot hope to be clear unless one is tolerably brief, I have often had to leave out qualifications that for accuracy's sake ought undoubtedly to have been made. But I have made no particular effort to steer away from controversy. For it is far better to stimulate disagreement than not to stimulate at all.

It now only remains to explain my choice of problem from which to start. The questions that are usually discussed under the heading of moral philosophy are probably linked together by tradition as much as by anything else. But there are two of them, on the answers to which will depend to one degree or another the answers that may be given to nearly all the rest. The first of these concerns the nature of value judgments as compared to other sorts of assertions, and in particular to statements of fact; the second, the existence or non-existence of free will and its bearing on notions of moral responsibility. Properly speaking these are not so much two questions as two groups of questions, and they are not in fact wholly independent of each other. When I was first trying to plan this book I had thought of dividing it into two approximately equal parts, one to each group of questions, with a linking chapter in between. But as I went on I found, inevitably no doubt, that the first part was growing so long that any book of which it were only a half would be of intolerable length. So what was first intended to be the linking chapter turns out to be the last full chapter of the book, in which I try only to show one of the ways in which the problem of value judgments can lead into the problem of free will, and to sketch in the barest of outlines some of the main issues with which this latter problem is bound up; and the book itself is in effect about the first group of problems only.

In these circumstances it could very reasonably be asked whether it may not be somewhat misleading to stick to the original title. For this problem of the nature of value judgments involves on the one hand some prior consideration of certain fundamental and very general issues concerning philosophy as a whole; while it is on the other hand a problem of which the nature of *moral* value judgments is after all but one aspect. For moral value judgments are by no means the only sort that are made. And I have indeed to admit that it is only in one chapter, and only in one part of that, that the problem of distinguishing moral from other values receives any explicit attention. All this on top of the fact that I have (in this book) little to say about freedom and not even a word about conscience.

But when all this has been admitted, it still seems to me that a discussion about the nature of value judgments can provide as good an introduction as any to moral philosophy. This is partly just because it does involve the incidental discussion of so many wider issues. For it would be a complete mistake to think of moral philosophy as a separate and self-contained subject of its own. A moral philosopher is one who is interested, certainly, in questions about moral judgments, but he must be in the first place a philosopher; and most philosophical problems turn out, if one pushes them far enough, to be involved in most others. It is true, similarly, that any discussion about the nature of value judgments is bound to have a bearing on a wide range of topics, only some of which will in themselves have anything to do with morals. On the other hand, the question of the nature of value judgments *is* of fundamental importance to moral philosophy. For anything that is true of value judgments in general must ipso facto hold for moral value judgments in particular; and if at the same time there are other implications too, then so much the better—it is a little like receiving a free sample along with the goods that one really went to purchase. As for the problem of marking off moral value judgments from the rest, it can surely only be tackled in the course of a general consideration of evaluation and not right at the outset. Finally, though it is also true, as I have already admitted, that there are very many topics which belong by tradition to moral philosophy but which make no appearance here, I can but repeat that this is intended as an introduction rather than as a survey— an introduction to a certain sort of approach, a certain style of argument, rather than to a certain range of opinions.

So the question for us now is, what is the nature of value judgments—on what may they be based and how do they differ from other sorts of judgments? Or at least this is the question in its most general aspect. In this very general and remote-seeming form, however, it would be very hard to tackle virtually out of the blue. It will be far better to start from one particular instance of the general problem, from the sort of question that might crop up in the course of some quite ordinary argument between people who find that they disagree on some matter of right or wrong, about whether someone or something is good or bad. Ninety-nine times out of a hundred we use these terms without the slightest hesitation, taking it for granted that we all know what each other means. And then, the hundredth time, an unexpectedly obstinate disagreement may suddenly give rise to doubt. You are sure that a certain sort of action is bad; but the man with whom you work is just as sure that it is good. It seems impossible that you should both be right, yet equally impossible for either to show that the other is wrong. Perhaps there has been a misunderstanding, perhaps you are talking at cross purposes, perhaps you do not really understand what each other wants to say. Perhaps even you may each become a little unsure of what you mean yourselves. It is at this sort of moment and in this sort of way that one may come to ask—what *does* it mean to say that something is good? This at any rate is the question with which we shall begin.

2

ON PROBLEMS OF DEFINITION

WHAT DOES IT mean to say of anything that it is good? It is hard to say at first glance whether this question is absurdly easy or absurdly difficult. Perhaps, in different ways, it is both. For most people would probably reply that they know perfectly well what they mean, but that they find it hard or impossible to express their meaning precisely. In a way there is nothing odd about this. It is notoriously one thing to do something that one knows how to do well, and very much another to explain exactly what it is that one is doing so that somebody else will be able to do it too; this is as true of using words correctly as it is of swimming or walking a tight rope. Indeed people hardly ever find it easy to explain exactly what any given word means. All the same, the word 'good' seems to present more of a puzzle than perhaps most of the others that we use. This is the more surprising in that so far from it being a technical term, it is on the contrary one of the commonest and most naturally used in the language.

The trouble is not that there are no suggestions available. It is on the contrary that there are so many that it is hard to see how they can all be compatible with each other. There is admittedly something unfair in pressing someone who is unwilling to commit himself to a definition of 'good'. When nevertheless, one is so unfair as to press people in this way, one meets again and again with answers such as these. 'Good', some say, means quite different things in each different context in which it is used, and perhaps even different things too to each person who uses it; thus for one person it will mean 'sweet and sparkling' when applied to cider, but 'short and clear' when applied to an argument; to another it may mean 'rough and still' and 'long and subtle'

9

B

when applied in the same two contexts. Others will prefer to distinguish two main senses, 'good as a means' and 'good as an end', where the first can be taken as roughly equivalent to 'efficient' and the second has to be left as incapable of further definition. Some say that its meaning is so vague that there is nothing useful that can be said about it beyond that it is employed to show some favourable reaction. Others that in its moral sense at least it has a definite meaning that can be understood, if they put their minds to it, by the great majority of people. Some, again, say something to the effect that anything that contributes to the general happiness is to that degree good; while others restrict themselves to the comment that one man's meat is another man's poison and that it is all a matter of taste.

It is possible, of course, that not all these answers, and the many others that are given, are so incompatible as they may sound. The notions of definition and meaning are themselves far from being so clear that we may expect a request for the meaning of a word always to be understood in the same way. Perhaps the most important point to settle whenever we are asked for definitions is whether we are being asked primarily about the usage of words or about the nature of things, because although sometimes roughly the same answer will do as well in either case, this is not always so. An example may help to make the distinction clear. Someone who is not familiar with the word, a child for instance, may ask me "What is 'green'?", and I may explain its meaning to him by pointing to different objects which are of that colour, while distinguishing them from others which are not. In this way he may learn to use the word for himself. Later on, however, the same child may be learning to paint and, knowing by now quite well how to use the word, may nevertheless ask me "What is green?", needing this time to know that it can be obtained by mixing blue and yellow. We may call the second empirical or factual information as opposed to the first which is linguistic. (The word 'empirical' means roughly 'relying on or derived from experience'. Clearly neither it nor the term 'factual' are altogether satisfactory for obviously there are facts about the language too. But they are often used to refer to something like 'non-linguistic experience' and 'the facts of the non-linguistic world' and therefore it is as well to introduce them in those senses here.) Notice how the nature of the information may depend on the circumstances in which it is offered. I might produce the same collection of green things that I showed to the child learning to control his vocabulary, to someone else who simply wanted to know what green things I had available. To such a person I shall evidently be giving empirical or factual information, to someone, moreover, who could not have asked for it correctly unless the *word* 'green' was already at his command.

It is true, of course, that there is often no clear line to be drawn between language and non-linguistic fact. Very naturally our theories and beliefs about the nature of things affect what comes to be the standard way of talking about them. Nevertheless it will often be useful to have a way of showing whether we are talking about language or the things to which we use language to refer.

Thus, while our theories and beliefs about the nature of things certainly affect what comes to be the standard way of talking about them, and while it is also true that it may be often impossible to draw a sharp line between language and non-linguistic fact and silly to attempt to do so, it will nevertheless be useful to have a way of showing which we are talking about. Indeed, if we had no clear method of marking the difference between using a part of our vocabulary in the normal manner on the one hand and talking about that vocabulary on the other, we should be in no position to discuss the problems of the relation between language and non-linguistic fact at all. There are a number of fashionable ways of marking this distinction, but it will be enough to introduce two of them here. Whenever we want to talk about any part of our language, be it a word or a phrase or any combination of phrases, we may set it aside in inverted commas; and a word set aside in this way we shall say we are *mentioning* rather than *using*. Thus the question "What is 'green'? " is a question about language—and notice now the double set of inverted commas, for not only is 'green' mentioned in the question, but the question itself I am mentioning as an example rather than using to ask for information. The question "What is green?", on the other hand, is a question about some matter of empirical fact.

Once we are in command of this distinction we may find that there are certain well-known paradoxical questions which can, for some purposes anyhow, be reduced to quite ordinary problems. The question "What is Nothing?", for example, has been felt by many to be full of dark and mysterious foreboding. The question "What is 'Nothing'?", a question as to the different possible ways of using the word, is of much less alarming proportions—though this does not mean to say that it is at once easy to answer. (It is interesting, incidentally, though again by no means easy, to consider the relation between these two different questions.)

There is one further terminological point. I propose to use the term 'definition' only in connection with matters of linguistic usage. It may be felt that this restriction is somewhat arbitrary in view of many past and present uses of the term. But it is a useful one, and in accord with most modern philosophical usage. For those for whom a slogan helps to fix such points in mind there is a well-known one at hand in "Definition is of words not of things". This slogan is less a statement of fact than the expression of a resolve to use the word 'definition' in a certain way.

Even if we confine our attention to definitions in the sense I have just laid down, there are still further important distinctions to be drawn. If I ask you about the meaning of a word, I may want to know about the way it is used in ordinary general language, about the way it is used by specialists in some more limited context or about the way in which you want it to be understood yourself, either in general or for some particular purpose; and there are other possibilities. Moreover, there are considerable differences in the types of answers for which these questions call. An account, for instance, of how a word is used in ordinary language may be found to be more or less accurate, more or less true or false. If true, it will be a statement of fact about language; for example, "In English 'a mare' means 'a female horse' ". (Once again it is worth noticing the use here of inverted commas. It happens that in English 'mare' does mean 'a female horse', but it might not have done and it might one day conceivably change. Words do change their meanings in the course of their histories and 'mare' means quite different things in some other languages. If, on the other hand, one leaves out the inverted commas and writes, "A mare is a female horse", one then has one of those curious assertions which are incontrovertibly true simply by virtue of the meanings of the terms employed. Such assertions are indeed puzzling in a number of ways; but we shall come back to this point in the next chapter.)

To return, however, to what we were saying about different types of definitions. Your account of how a word is used in ordinary language, then, may turn out to be more or less accurate just like any other account which has to report certain facts. This is also true of any account you may offer of how a word is used in some more specialised context, by biologists, for example. What about the case where you are asked for your own usage of a term? Here there are at least two distinct possibilities. Somebody may want to know how you personally are accustomed to use a certain word; and in this case the situation is like the two mentioned above in that your reply may be, depending on your memory and your truthfulness, a more or less accurate reflection of the facts. It may be, on the other hand, that what is wanted is that you make up your mind how you propose to use the term in question from now on, that you cease to be so vague or that you choose between two or

13

more incompatible usages. Often, indeed, you may wish to introduce some new and precise usage for the purposes you have in mind without first being asked to do so by anyone else. Here a decision is called for and a decision is in important ways unlike a statement of fact. It can, for instance, be good or bad, depending on the purposes you have, but it can not appropriately be said to be true or false. If your statement of general usage turns out to be wrong, you may be accused of a deliberate attempt to mislead, but more probably of a lack of knowledge; you may equally be accused of a deliberate attempt to mislead if the way in which you continue to talk seems incompatible with the intentions that you have declared, but this time you will hardly be accused of ignorance, rather of a lack of grasp or of a tiresome tendency to lapse into inconsistency and muddles. To use a word now in one way, now in another may be highly confusing but it is not in itself to say anything false.

In all contexts where there is a special need for clarity, consistency is indeed essential. Except on those comparatively rare occasions where one actually intends to be misleading, there can be no point in laying down or stipulating a certain usage unless it is scrupulously adhered to. In fact, it can often be worse to fail to stick to a rule once one has laid it down than not to have laid down any rule at all, for where it is clear that ordinary everyday language is being used in an ordinary everyday way, people are less likely to go wrong looking for precise meanings where there are none to be found. This is actually one of the main features of ordinary language, many of whose terms are used in a variety of different ways, some of which bear no very obvious resemblance to each other. No doubt, it is probably true that if we could assemble all the different usages of a term, we should very often be able to trace some sort of relation of family likeness linking them together. But since some usages of a term, like some members of a family, tend to die out and become forgotten, leaving great gaps in the chain of family likeness, we may be obliged to consult a historian of language in order to be sure whether we are dealing with what is by origin one word or two. (For those engaged in any linguistic study, philology or grammar and so on, the question of what criteria to choose on which to base the usage of the term 'a word' provides in point of fact a particularly interesting and difficult exercise in the problem of definition.) Nor, for most of the terms of ordinary language, can any very precise limits be laid down for their different usages. We may know the difference between green and blue without being sure as to where one shades into the other. Even if we attempt to reduce the area of uncertainty by introducing the terms 'greenish-blue' and 'blueish-green', we may still find, as we in fact do, that there are cases where we have no general rules by which to decide whether to use one of these terms or the other. This inherent vagueness or indeterminacy of ordinary language will seldom matter very much, for the borderline cases may be very rare or unimportant for the purposes in hand; and anyhow there is a good deal that can be done by proper arrangement of our terms to reduce their occurrence. But if we are sufficiently worried by them to want to try and cut them out altogether, there seems to be nothing to be done but to base the terms in question on some accurately measurable quantities; in the case of colours, for example, on the wave-lengths of light. The trouble is that if we do this we virtually take the terms out of ordinary language and introduce them into some scientific theory; and we shall still want some way of talking about colours as we see them, for our eyes are not instruments for the measuring of light waves[1].

---

[1] The difference there is here between scientific and non-scientific language may be illustrated by the fact that in languages with different colour classifications from English—whose colour terms, that is to say, cannot be exactly translated into our colour terms, because the two do not exactly correspond to each other—the borderline cases will crop up at quite different points of the spectrum, while the nature

For these reasons, while a stipulated definition is likely to be better the less ambiguous that it is, it will generally be a mistake to look for one clear-cut meaning of a term of ordinary language which is to do for all possible cases. This, it may be felt, is a very trivial and obvious point, which everybody knows already. But it is worth insisting on. Many people, for instance, seem to think that there are difficult practical problems that could be settled if only one could discover the 'real' meaning of some key word, irrespective of any particular purpose or context. Under different usages of a term such as 'man', those perhaps of the biologist and the lawyer, they may look for some fundamental but as yet unused usage of which these two, and many others, must be but variants. And how often does one come across people trying to support their arguments by insisting that "This is the real meaning of the word 'so-and-so' "—'democracy' or 'freedom', for example. Such a claim may sometimes be equivalent to "This is the original usage of the term" or "This is the way the great majority of people use it most of the time", but very often it is less like any sort of statement than a recommendation in favour of some particular theory or point of view. Thus one might find somebody, who for some reason wished everyone to do as much of their thinking as possible in terms of physics, insisting that the real meaning of the word 'energy' was that the physicists give to it. Or to take the more familiar example, one can find speakers on either side, who may expound in clear factual terms the working differences between communist and capitalist society,

---

of the spectrum itself will, it goes without saying, remain the same. Nor is any real analogy to be found in the fact that problems as to what is to count as fair experimental error can arise in the taking of scientific measurements. The use of a fundamentally numerical system of terms can be determined independently of their application in particular instances, however difficult their application may turn out to be. The very use, or meaning, of terms for simple sense experiences, on the other hand, can only be determined by reference to the experiences as they present themselves.

nevertheless determined to show that only one of the two is entitled to the (honourable) name of 'democracy'. But, in the short run anyhow, the name you give the facts does nothing to change them[1]; though, such is the power of language, it may quite well change your own and other people's attitudes and through them the future course of events. It is sometimes possible to persuade children, small and not so small, to take a medicine for which they have a declared dislike by telling them that it is a new kind of sweet; and water, suitably and impressively labelled, is an old and often successful prescription of doctors.

To sum up, then. All definition, as we shall use the term, is of words and not of things. Stipulative definitions, that is to say usages that may be laid down for certain specific purposes, cannot, unlike statements, be said to be true or false, though they may certainly be effective or ineffective. Any deductive system, such as a geometry for example, is full of definitions of this type. Definitions which, on the other hand, purport to give an account either of general or of specialised usage are statements of a certain sort of fact. In some limited contexts, it may be possible to give definitions of very great precision; this is so in scientific or legal discourse, for instance. As far as everyday language is concerned, however, there is need of considerable caution. In many cases, indeed, we may be able to put forward short and unambiguous statements of meaning, which may well hold true within wide general limits. But it is better to treat them as guides, as which they may be extremely useful, than as standards to which all usage must, on pain of being meaningless, conform. Moreover, the realisation that there is no particular reason to suppose that there must be one

[1] I do not want to imply there is some way of getting at the pure facts independently of the language that must be used to talk or even to think about them. The exact relationship between language and fact is a very difficult and controversial matter; for, as we have already noted, there is no neat line to be drawn between language and the non-linguistic world. However there is no need to worry over subleties of this kind in the present context.

general rule for the meaning of a given term releases one from the temptation to keep on rejecting such general rules as we have found whenever we run across exceptions.

We seem to have moved a good way in this chapter from the question with which we began it. But there is no real need to apologise. Questions of meaning are always tricky and if our answers are to be free of confusions, we must be clear as to the conditions under which such answers are possible. Or at least as clear as we can be; for anything like a full examination of these background questions would take us far too far off our course.

3

ON STATEMENTS, SYNTHETIC AND ANALYTIC

PEOPLE often suppose, of course, that it is the business of moral philosophers to discover, if they can, the real nature of virtue or of goodness; in some more or less confused way they are thought of as teachers of how to live. But if, after all, to ask what it means to say of anything that it is 'good' is to be taken simply as a question about the meaning of a word, why, you may ask, should one go to a philosopher rather than to a dictionary for the answer? It has indeed been suggested more than once that if only a really adequate dictionary were provided, philosophers would be freed to go and do something else[1]; and some unkind critics have observed that the conclusion which certain modern philosophers have come to, by way of considerable controversy and argument, that the word 'good' is used to commend, would have been reached with much less trouble had they consulted the Oxford English Dictionary where 'good' is described as 'the most general term of commendation in the English language'. This incidentally, is an alternative that I left out of my list at the beginning of the previous chapter. But even if this criticism is accepted, certain questions will remain. Why have philosophers been taking such a perversely long way round? Why, if the dictionary solution is so obvious, should so many other different and apparently conflicting answers be given by ordinary non-philosophic people—(as they are, for none of the answers in that list have I invented myself)?

In fact, of course, apparently simple and harmless

---

[1] Some philosophers themselves have believed and believe that their business is essentially to provide such a dictionary.

questions about the meanings of words, may raise issues of quite general and fundamental importance. A very good example of the apparently by the way questions over which philosophers have been concerned in the course of their discussion about the meaning of 'good' is whether a moral judgment can be expressed in some kind of statement and, if not, why not. This is a typical philosophers' problem and may seem excessively academic and remote; but its implications are anything but that. Let me try to explain.

Many people say, and many more, perhaps, would want to, that all standards of value depend in the last resort on certain moral truths; that there are some things which are right or wrong, good or bad, in themselves, irrespective of what anyone may think or do about them; that cruelty, to take an instance, which has no other end than itself, is not merely undesirable but is positively wrong. What is the force of this 'positively wrong'? It is sometimes expressed by saying that the wrongness of such cruelty is absolute or intrinsic or objective. These three terms are not exactly equivalent and can be bound up in a complicated manner with various more or less different theories; but the point remains the simple one that if cruelty is wrong, it is wrong because of what it is and not because of anyone's views on the subject. On the contrary, whether or not a man's views on the subject are true or false will depend on whether he properly understands the nature of cruelty. This way of looking at the matter has, of course, been contested often enough, but to those who have disagreed with it the reply has generally been that if there were no objective moral standards, to condemn such things as cruelty would amount to no more than to express a personal distaste; and that though on proper reflection this is quite unbelievable, if and when it should generally be taken seriously, the common standards of behaviour would be bound to suffer a disastrous decline.

Be that as it may, it is undeniable that most people can at times be found arguing about their judgments of value as if their truth or falsity did directly depend on the nature of the things or events under discussion, or, which comes to the same thing for the objectivity of moral standards, the nature of their eventual consequences. We must, moreover, try to avoid any confusion over the sense of this much used but not very satisfactory term 'objectivity'. For some people have argued that since the standards which any individual will instinctively accept are set not by himself alone but by the community, past and present, in which he finds himself and are thus independent of his personal feelings, they are for him as objective as they could possibly be. But to argue in this way is to miss the point of the claim that in saying that cruelty is wrong, one is saying something about cruelty itself. This cannot be equivalent to expressing or associating oneself with the likes and dislikes of the community, still less, as has been foolishly suggested on occasions, to saying what those likes and dislikes are. Most at any rate of the people who call themselves objectivists do so because of their claim that the truth or falsity of moral judgments depends wholly on the nature of the *objects* which they are about and not on the subject who makes them—nor, for that matter, on any number of subjects.

What has all this to do with the notion of statement? The answer is straight-forward enough. A statement may generally be understood to be any expression capable of being true or false. And if this is right it must follow that anyone who holds that there is a good firm sense in which moral judgments (which form, of course, a very important class of those judgments which may involve the use of words like 'good'), may be true or false, is in effect maintaining that they come under the category of statements.

This may be worth some expansion. To say that a statement is 'any expression capable of being true or false' is undoubtedly to lay oneself open to certain routine objections; a more cautious way of putting it might be to say that 'a statement is an assertion for which one can think of some way, in theory at least, of bringing reason to show that

21

it is probably true or false'. (Imperatives, for instance, are not statements, as the words 'true' and 'false' can no more be applied to them than they can to signs of pleasure or to grunts of annoyance.) But the underlying point is that the words 'true', 'false' and 'statement' all belong to the same general family; the use of any one of these terms commits one, if challenged, to certain usages of the others. For example, it would normally be considered senseless to say that one was making a statement but to deny at the same time that it might be true or false or anything in between; to do this would be to withdraw one of the main rules which govern our usage of this term without substituting any other to take its place.

There may, on the other hand, be occasions where one needs to alter or refine a rule of language in this way; and the discussions which have taken place between logicians as to the best way of classifying an assertion like "The 1954 King of France is bald" provide an excellent illustration of such possibilities. Bertrand Russell took the line that this is a statement and a false statement at that, arguing that it is equivalent to the assertion of a conjunction of three statements, one of which is "There is a King of France in 1954". Since there is no problem in saying that this latter statement is false and since no matter how many members of a conjunction of statements are true when taken singly, if one is false so is the whole conjunction as a group, it follows that "The 1954 King of France is bald" is false. To some people, however, it may seem too artificial to analyse this apparently straightforward assertion as a conjunction of three others and Mr. Strawson has preferred to say that as it refers to nothing it is neither true nor false but empty. Well, then, you may ask, in that case is it to be counted as a statement? The answer is that we may say that it is, introducing 'empty through lack of reference' as a third alternative to 'true' and 'false'; or we may stick to our former rule and say that it would have been one had it only referred to something. Which we say does not matter in itself and will depend on the commitments we want to enter into as far as the other words in the group in which we are interested are concerned. But the general moral is that whatever we do, we can never, when doubtful, proceed with the use of a word before seeing how all the others belonging to the same group will be affected, without risk of running into inconsistencies and consequent failure to achieve any clear meaning. The particular moral is that if for any reason we wish to disassociate the words 'true' and 'false' on the one hand and 'statement' on the other, we must be careful to set out in detail exactly what we are doing together with our reasons for doing it if we are not to leave the situation hopelessly imprecise.

The main point is, however, that if one wants to say that one's moral judgments can be either true or false, or if one wants to maintain that there are fundamental moral truths, one must in the first place consider whether these judgments can justifiably be called statements. For if they cannot, there is at least on the surface something odd in talking of moral truths. This is so important a matter that in an effort to clarify the situation I propose to give the rest of the chapter to a further consideration of the term 'statement' alone.

In order to do this we shall need to introduce a limited number of technical terms. For it has by now become common philosophic practice to classify all statements or propositions—a term also frequently used by logicians, which for our purposes we may take as synonomous with 'statements'—under the two heads of 'synthetic' and 'analytic'; and these two terms are very widely employed as tools of analysis and discussion. Originally, as a matter of fact, they were brought into use by philosophers who talked of judgments rather than of propositions or statements in all contexts and not only where values were concerned. At the same time they accepted the traditional view that all propositions or judgments were made up of subject and predicate. If, according to them, the predicate of a judgment was discoverable simply through analysis of the subject, then the judgment was analytic; if, however, the predicate could not be obtained by any amount of such analysis, then it was synthetic. "Grey squirrels tend to oust red squirrels" would be an example of a synthetic judgment; since simply by analysing the notions of 'red', 'grey' and 'squirrel' one would never be able to settle which, if either, would tend to oust the other. The judgment "Every effect has a cause", on the other hand, would be said to be analytic on the grounds that the idea of 'cause' is already contained in the very idea of 'effect' (and, indeed, vice versa); an uncaused effect is unthinkable, a mere contradiction in terms. The result of such an analysis of the subject of a judgment might in practice appear surprising, but there is a sense, it was held, in which an analytic judgment would bring no new information. To anyone who had properly understood the subject—and if it were a very complex one, one could always postulate a perfect intelligence such as that of God—the explicit setting out of the results of analysis in the full subject predicate form would be superfluous. A synthetic judgment, on the other hand, was so called because in it were brought and held together two ideas basically independent of each other, neither of them, that is to say, being contained in the other. In this case the information contained in the judgment could be said to be new in that no amount of pure analysis of the subject could have led to its discovery prior to the establishment by independent means of the judgment's truth. If one wanted to know which kind of squirrels, if either, tended to oust the other, one would have to go and make actual observations in the woods and fields.

Recent philosophers have, however, given up this way of making the distinction. This is partly because they have come to regard the term 'judgment' as imprecise and equivocal and responsible for a number of confusions; partly because it is no longer thought to be necessary or

24

even appropriate to look for the subject-predicate division in every possible sort of proposition—in some cases, indeed, to force a proposition into this mould may not only be pointless, it may be positively misleading; and partly because talk about the predicate 'being contained' in the subject and about the analysis of concepts has come to seem to be of too metaphorical a kind to lend itself to any very exact investigation. For how is one to decide whether a given predicate is contained in a given subject or not, and with what sort of tools is one to set about the analysis of concepts? So for one reason and another, and not least because many of the thinkers concerned had a strong interest in mathematics and logic and consequently in the nature of symbols, it was felt best to make the distinction in the context of a study of language as a means of communication[1]. By dealing with words and sentences, statements and propositions, rather than with concepts and judgments, it was hoped that it would be easier to see exactly where one was.

In fact this hope was somewhat over optimistic and, surprisingly or not according to one's point of view, it has still proved difficult to agree on the best way of making the distinction. To indicate its nature, however, without committing oneself to a rigorous definition, is by no means so hard; and indeed we have already just touched on the subject in the preceding chapter. Roughly, then, we may say that an *analytic* proposition is one whose truth or falsity depends on the meaning of one or more of the words it contains; while the truth or falsity of a *synthetic* proposition depends on the actual nature of the facts which the proposition claims to be about. In terms of the examples we have just taken, the truth of "Every effect has a cause" can be checked by analysis of the rules governing the meanings of the terms 'effect' and 'cause', while if you want to verify that grey squirrels tend to oust red squirrels you will have, as we said, to find out what happens in the

---

[1] Not, for instance, as a means of self-expression or of common ritual.

woods and fields. The truth of an analytic proposition can be known, it is said, *a priori*, that is without having to consider anything outside the terms of the proposition itself; but if a proposition is synthetic, its truth or falsity can only be discovered *a posteriori*, that is to say by an examination of the way things are, further to any study of what the proposition itself may mean. If an analytic proposition is true, it is, given the rules of language, *necessarily* so—(a proposition that is analytically false, for example "Not every effect has a cause", is usually called a contradiction). But whether a synthetic proposition is true or false, it is always logically possible that the opposite should have been the case; for since its truth is not guaranteed by language, it must be at least meaningful to put forward its contradictory. As opposed to necessary, a synthetic proposition is said to be *contingent* by which is meant that its truth or falsity is contingent on the way the world happens to be.

There is one other point about terminology which should perhaps be made clear. The way in which I have just used the phrase 'logically possible' is a semi-technical one and not altogether in accord with the way in which it is used, by some people at any rate, in ordinary speech. In the sense in which I am using the term, to say that a suggestion is logically possible is simply to say that it is not self-contradictory; it is to say, that is, that the suggestion, however fanciful, is at least clearly meaningful. (Logicians are concerned with meaningful, not practical possibilities.) In any practical sense I take it as being quite beyond the bounds of possibility that the next time the cows come into the field at the bottom of my garden, they should link tails and sing 'Old Lang Syne' in a broad Scottish accent. But the proposition in which I have put forward the suggestion is a synthetic proposition. The suggestion is thus both meaningful and logically possible. It is logically impossible (self-contradictory) that anyone should draw a square circle. The logical impossibility is neither greater nor less whether it be a cow or a mathematician whom I suggest should draw this figure. Logical impossibilities are not matters of more or less.

The last two paragraphs have, I am afraid, seen the introduction of an uncomfortable number of new technical or semi-technical terms, but again it is important that they should be familiar if the course of recent philosophic discussion is to be understood. For one of the central controversies that have been carried on has been the question whether or not the truth of any synthetic propositions can be discovered *a priori*. Put in such a dry manner it may well seem that the interest of the problem could hardly extend beyond the most abstracted of academic circles; but this would be a false impression.

We have seen that the truth of an analytic proposition, or statement, can, in principle be established without the need to make even the simplest of empirical observations; it follows that whatever we may observe can make no difference to the truth of such a proposition[1]. Take, for example, the proposition "Anyone who makes nought at cricket, makes a duck". One can see at once that this is an analytic proposition, because its truth follows immediately from the meanings in this context of the words 'nought' and 'duck'; and so can be established by reference to the language of cricket, without any need to wait for somebody actually to score nought and see what happens then. But it is not just that there is no need to go and watch cricket matches to establish this truth; there could be no point in doing so. No matter how many cricket matches one attended, one would and could never come across a case of a man making nought without making a duck. There is no score whatsoever that a batsman might make that could make any difference to this sad and simple truth. And one knows this in advance, precisely because it is analytic. But if,

[1] Observations may, of course, serve as a check on propositions that have been derived from faulty analysis or, in complicated cases, suggest the discovery of new ones that can be validly derived. The point is that if the analysis is correctly carried out, observations are neither needed nor capable of making any difference.

quite generally, the truth of an analytic proposition is compatible with any result of any kind of observation about the state of the world that we might care to make, then it can exclude no possible state of affairs and fails, therefore, to tell us anything about the observable world at all. Although it is true that if I make nought, then I shall make a duck, this fortunately provides no basis for predicting what score I shall in fact make. For any genuine information about the world we must turn in the end to synthetic propositions; on this point there has been extremely little disagreement. But when all these terms were being introduced in the preceeding paragraph, you will have noticed that 'analytic', 'necessary' and '*a priori*' fell on one side of the fence and 'synthetic', 'contingent' and '*a posteriori*' on the other. If, therefore, this division is allowed to pass without challenge, it must follow that nothing can be known about the world independently of the taking of observations—which is, incidentally, the main contention of all empiricist philosophies. For, let it be repeated, to say that a proposition is *a posteriori* is to say that the truth of what it asserts depends on a state of affairs which can only be discovered with the aid of observations; while to say that it is contingent is to emphasise the aspect that there is always a sense in which such facts might have been otherwise, for no observations would be needed if it could have been shown by other considerations alone that the facts could be only one way. So anyone who wishes to maintain that there are some things that can be known about the world, things, that is to say, which are genuinely informative, which will hold true whatever experience might bring, is bound in effect to maintain the possibility of synthetic *a priori* propositions; synthetic on the first count, *a priori* on the second.

Nobody would pretend that it is easy to see how propositions can in fact be at the same time synthetic and *a priori*, not even those who believe such a thing to be possible; which indeed it is not if the terms are to be understood in some such way as I have suggested. I shall come back to this point very shortly. But meanwhile it is worth emphasising that though there may be disagreements over whether 'synthetic' and '*a priori*' are compatible terms, '*a priori*' and 'necessary' in these contexts always go together. This is because the issue concerns how a proposition can be known to be true, not how it may come to be thought of in the first place. We may be sceptical or we may not if someone claims to have had information revealed to him from a non-empirical source, but provided he admits the possibility that his information might be incorrect, no objection can be made to his claim on purely logical grounds[1]. However you may hit on the answer to a problem, by guesswork or by some other means, no protest will be raised if you are prepared to have your solution checked against the facts. As we have just seen, a proposition can be known to be necessarily true only if we can show that whatever curious things might start to happen in the world, there would still be no observation by which it could be upset. It is about the possibility of *a priori* knowledge in this strong sense that all the arguments have taken place.

There are a number of different people who, for one reason or another, might want to claim the possibility of incontrovertible knowledge, including certain moral philosophers. But before turning back to them and to the proper subject of our discussion, we should just mention the case of the metaphysicians, as it was they who provoked the most systematic and best-known attack on this line of thought. It is, of course, naughty to use the term 'metaphysicians' in this way, for if it is not being employed merely as a term of abuse, it calls for considerable explanation which this is not the place to give. But one way of regarding the activities of many of those who would traditionally have received this title is to think of them as those of an armchair scientist, who claims to produce from his armchair

[1] We might have to accept certain qualifications to this remark if we were to go into this question in very much greater and more careful detail than seems necessary here.

theories of the most general and profound significance as to the nature of the world. Experimental scientists do often tend to be suspicious of armchair scientists as such. But that a theory comes from the armchair is in itself nothing against it; no one would suggest that theoretical physicists, for example, are not genuinely occupied in science. What is essential, however, is, as scientists are continually telling us, that the theory should in principle at least be open to test. This, it appeared, was precisely what was the matter with nearly all metaphysical theories; they were too securely based. For if a theory is proof against *any* possible counter-example, if nothing whatsoever that happened could make any difference to its truth or falsity, then it must share the characteristic of analytic propositions of telling us nothing at all of the world we experience. Such theories, it has been widely thought and with much evident reason, can neither help forward scientific research nor constitute part of the body of scientific knowledge; they can only get in the way. While they might be harmless enough for those who like that sort of large-scale speculation, they are something from which any person with a concern for genuine scientific enquiry must keep scrupulously clear[1]. The trouble is that it is often by no means obvious at first sight when and whether a theory becomes vacuous in this way or not, and even the most would-be-empirical of scientists may sometimes be misled by failure to recognise for what it is, a theory that is at bottom untestable. Because of this it seemed important to a number of thinkers to set up some criterion by means of which it might be possible to decide whether a theory had some empirical content or whether it was so hedged about with qualifications as to render it empty.

This is the origin, in one of its forms at any rate, of the so-called Principle of Verification, which has attained a certain general notoriety. To start with the notion of

[1] But once again there are serious qualifications to be made. See note (1), p. 36.

verification was required simply to serve as the criterion by which genuine hypotheses could be distinguished from those that were empty or bogus. If it was possible to say what sort of observations would be or would have been needed to confirm the theory, this showed that it was a genuine one and empirical in nature—that is to say, with some genuine relation to possible experience. The fact that there might be no known means of actually making the observations necessary to test the theory was from this point of view neither here nor there[1]. Even in the days when it still seemed beyond all possibility to go and have a look at the other side of the moon, people could say what sorts of observations *would* establish that there were ranges of mountains there. So this suggestion was and is an empirically meaningful one, quite apart from considerations of rockets and space travel. If, on the other hand, it turned out that a theory was able to accommodate any and every result of any and every conceivable experiment, it could clearly provide no basis on which to predict that such and such would occur *rather than* something else. By allowing for every possibility, it would succeed in asserting none. This criterion of verifiability is based obviously enough directly on such considerations as to the nature of empirical, scientific assertions. It is true that some people have in fact objected to talking of verification in such contexts on the grounds that although scientists may often reject theories as a result of the outcome of one or more experiments, there is an important sense in which no theory can ever be completely verified. But this does not matter either. One could as well talk of a falsification as of a verification theory of meaning; and some in fact have preferred to do so. All that is essential is that one must be able to say what would count for the theory and what would count against it. Which simply comes back to saying that the statement of any

---

[1] But—as an added complication—it may not always be clear at first sight whether the impossibility of making observations is in fact of a practical or of a theoretical nature.

genuine theory must contain at least one proposition that is synthetic—(and not *a priori*).

It was in this way that the challenge to the 'metaphysicians' was thrown down. If they wanted their theories to be taken seriously, they must be prepared to show what difference they made, to specify, that is to say, the conditions under which they might be shown to be false. If their theories were to be empirically meaningful, they could not be necessarily true; if they were to be necessarily true, they could have no relation to any type of experience. It was impossible to have it both ways. One could not, in short, have propositions that were both synthetic and *a priori*. If what was alleged to be a proposition could not be classified as either analytic or synthetic, then it was not a proposition at all; it was but meaningless nonsense, Once this distinction was firmly grasped, the achievements of science would, it was hoped, be much clarified and advanced.

It is, of course, one thing to produce a criterion to enable the recognition of empirically significant generalisations and very much another to evolve a whole theory of meaning and there is no doubt that many exponents of this method overstated their claims in a manner that was, to say the least, highly misleading. It may be perhaps that a new theory can sometimes only make its mark by an original overstatement. But this, in any case, is not the place to trace the history of the notion of verification. There is, all the same, one point that is worthy of further note. The verificationists were originally concerned with propositions purporting to give general information about the world, particularly information of a possible scientific interest— about space or time, for example. But the criterion they produced will, it seems, very naturally do duty as a test for any proposition purporting to give factual information, whether it be general or not. If this broadens the possible field of application, however, it at the same time broadens it for any possible counter-attack. For it would need only one synthetic *a priori* proposition to be found, however uninteresting it might be in itself, for the whole case against the possibility of invulnerable knowledge to be overthrown. It appeared to many of them, therefore, that each fresh candidate put forward for the position of synthetic *a priori* proposition must receive specific analysis and be shown to be a false pretender. So though it is doubtless true that many practising philosophers are carried away by their love of ingenuity and the joys of the analytical chase, the fact that in each particular instance a whole philosophical position seemed at stake may make more intelligible the lengthy discussions that have taken place of many otherwise somewhat curious problems. It should also make more intelligible, as we shall notice later, the treatment meted out to ethical 'propositions' by the earlier Logical Positivists.

I must add, however, that in my view the seriousness of these discussions has sometimes seemed very misplaced. I have two main reasons for this, neither of them particularly original. The first of these I have in fact already referred to in passing. It concerns the way in which I introduced the terms 'synthetic' and 'analytic', not in connection with the older language of subject, predicate and concept but in the context of a study of the meanings of words and phrases. It follows from the type of usage that they are given in this latter context that if a proposition is *a priori*, it can only be analytic. (It could be said that that there is no synthetic *a priori* is itself an analytic proposition.) The reason for this is that a proposition is only counted as synthetic if it excludes some logically possible state of affairs and this is enough to render it *a posteriori*; if it fails to do this, it is analytic—or empty of any type of meaning and not to be counted as a genuine proposition at all. Thus the exclusiveness of the distinction between 'analytic' and 'synthetic' and their associated terms on either side of the fence follows from a linguistic decision. But it should not be thought that such a decision must have been either obvious or arbitrary. On the contrary, the reasons for dissatisfaction with the old Kantian way of making the distinction are often extremely intricate and are still quite often disputed; which is not, in fact, surprising since the way one deals with these particular matters is fundamental to one's whole view of philosophy. At any rate, to cut what could be a very long story short, a great number of philosophers have, in their own different ways, concluded that only definitions of some such type as those I have suggested can in the end lead to clear thinking on these subjects. My only point here is simply that once one does come to a general decision that the terms in question must be understood in this sort of way, there need be no very great anxiety about the possible emergence of particular counter-examples.

This does not mean that the distinction can be applied readily and neatly to any and every proposition and that there will be no borderline cases. Indeed, that is what nearly all the well-known candidates for the title of synthetic *a priori* are. With sufficient ingenuity, however, they can always be pushed in one direction or the other. In any case, whatever happens, the reasons that can be produced for calling such a proposition synthetic are bound at the same time to be reasons for denying that it is *a priori* and vice versa. Which way the push will actually go will depend on what is taken for granted as to the general background of facts, as to the meanings to be attached to the key words concerned and even as to what is to be counted as a proposition. One might, for example, want to say that the proposition "One cannot be in Oban and Crewe at the same time" is analytically true by virtue of the use that is given to these two place names or, on the other hand, that its truth depends on the contingent fact that nobody is large enough to have one foot in each camp; (I am deliberately bypassing the complications of the phrase 'at the same time' as irrelevant for the purposes of illustration). Or consider the sentence "The author of this sentence is a user of language". It is not logically impossible that it should be 'written' by the wind in the desert sand; but, if this flight of imagination is to be taken seriously at all, should such marks be counted as constituting a proposition, and, if so, as one that was true or false?

This brings me to my second main reason. It is surely wrong to suppose that a proposition is something which has some sort of independent existence and whose nature can be determined by a careful scrutiny without reference to any particular context. Different people may use the same words differently and the same person too may use the same words, and sentences, with different purposes on different occasions; often, of course, the range of variations may be very wide indeed. This makes it extremely hard to pin down propositions, of ordinary language at any rate, for clinical examination at all. The case may be different in more specialised contexts, because we may there find the key terms governed by much stricter and more uniform rules, which make the occurrence of borderline propositions correspondingly less probable—though even here still not impossible. Indeed, at least one leading modern philosopher has been so impressed by the looseness of the terms 'meaning' and 'sameness of meaning' as to regard the distinction between 'analytic' and 'synthetic' as to all intents and purposes useless.

There is no need, however, to go as far as that. This pair of terms with the other members of their family can still be most helpful, provided that we treat them not as labels for use with some all-inclusive logical filing cabinet, but as tools of analysis to be brought out on particular occasions. Whenever it is uncertain what exactly some apparent statement means or from where some impressive generalisation really gets its strength, it is a fair and useful challenge, to oneself as well as to others, to demand a clear decision whether what is being asserted is analytic or synthetic; if synthetic, what are the possibilities excluded, if analytic, what are the precise usages intended of the terms on which all depends? This is not to say that we must at all times pause before speaking to decide that our statements are definitely one or the other—indeed, to insist upon this would be to rule out nearly all imaginative advance even in scientific fields—but only that we must make up our minds if and when we wish to ensure a definite statement. For while we may fairly reply that we are not sure whether what we are saying is analytic or synthetic, we can not reply that it is neither one nor the other and still claim that it is clearly informative[1]. Thus I do not at all want to suggest that to experiment with various possible pushes may not be illuminating in any particular instance; on the contrary, it may be very well worth while to lay bare the main alternatives, depending, obviously enough, on the nature and importance of the problem.

There is one loose end to be dealt with before we finish with this section. The question is implicit in much of what we have been saying in this chapter whether we are justified in treating analytic and synthetic statements as being on a par at all. This point came up in the last chapter with regard to the proposition "A mare is a female horse". If we had put in the inverted commas to show that we were mentioning the term ' "mare" '[2] rather than using it and written instead " A 'mare' means 'a female horse' ", then there would have been no problem; we should have had a synthetic proposition, which is in fact true (if it is intended to be about the English language)—though, of course, it is logically possible that it might not have been. But, given

---

[1] But though clarity is a great thing, it is, of course, in the words of Professor Price, not always enough. The fruitfulness of a new generalisation may often lie precisely in its uncertain application; if its limits were hard, fast and indisputable, it might be far less suggestive. On the whole, the emphasis on clarity in all matters *at all times* has come from those more interested either in mathematics or in the statement of the results of natural science rather than in its possible further revolutions. Both sides obviously are needed and depend greatly on each other.

[2] The reason for the double set of inverted commas is that I am here *mentioning*—in order to talk about it itself—the symbol which I earlier *used* to talk about something else; namely the word which we used for a female horse.

this fact about language, the corresponding analytic proposition is incontrovertibly true; its truth follows, in the familiar way, from the very meaning of the term employed. The question is, what can it be about? Since, given these facts of language, there is no possible occurrence with which it is incompatible, it is what we have called vacuous and provides no information about anything. Thus there is, it is clear, a strong temptation to say that analytic propositions are about nothing whatever. Indeed the most common occurrence of analytic propositions in the ordinary course of affairs[1] is when people get into a muddle and think they are saying something impressive when in fact they are not. (Or they may intend to muddle their audience by seeming to say something important when they know perfectly well they are not.) But if analytic propositions are about nothing, why should we single them out from other vacuous assertions as a genuine type of proposition?

Part of the answer may be given by referring to tradition. Another part doubtless lies in the fact that there is a large class of what are usually taken to be analytic propositions the importance of whose role is not to be disputed by even the most puritanical of empiricists, namely the formulae and theorems of mathematics. These it would be absurd to treat as would-be statements, which had tried but failed to achieve any empirical content. If it comes to that, of course, there are many other types of assertion which it would be equally absurd to treat in this way. But mathematics is of obvious and overriding importance to science and it is on science that so many empiricists have had their attention fixed. Even so there have been plenty of arguments over the best way of describing the nature of analytic propositions; but to cut a long story short, it again does not particularly matter, for present purposes anyhow, what we choose to say provided only that we are aware of what the situation is and are consistent in the way we decide to talk about it.

Those who are interested in this point might like to look at the article on 'Analytic Truths' by D. W. Hamlyn in '*Mind*' July 1956.

The essential point is that the truth or falsity of analytic and synthetic propositions are to be decided in very different ways; in the one case by reference to the rules of the language or symbolic system to which the proposition belongs—or to the establishing of such rules if there is as yet no hard and fast usage; in the other case by means of some observation, systematised and refined as the context may demand. To this dictum there seems to be one class of exceptions, namely synthetic statements about language, since the type of observation by which their truth or falsity will be determined must involve what I have just called a reference to the rules of language. Perhaps the best thing to say will be that while a synthetic proposition about some matter of language actually states that the rules are such and such, an analytic proposition simply gives expression to such a rule or, as in nearly all the more important cases, to some indirect consequence of one or more rules taken together.

Let me try to summarise this not very easy chapter. We started by suggesting that for many people, whatever they may feel about the dictionary definition of 'good' as the 'most general term of commendation', its use in moral contexts is bound up with the idea of objective moral truths; truths, that is to say, which are wholly independent of what anyone may do or think, whoever they might be. The notions of 'true' and 'false', however, are in their turn bound up with the notion of 'statement' (or 'proposition'). Partly because this latter term is unlike 'truth' in not being the centre of very strong emotions and therefore easier to tackle in the first instance, partly because a certain familiarity with the terms 'analytic' and 'synthetic' is essential if modern philosophical discussion of any sort is to be followed, we turned for the rest of the chapter to a consideration of this traditional classification of statements.

The modern way of using these terms is, as in the case of 'definition', linked to a study of language. As a rough indication of their usage, we said that an analytic proposition can be discovered to be true or false simply by reference to the meanings of the terms it contains, while the truth or falsity of a synthetic proposition depends on the state of the 'facts'. Analytic propositions are *a priori* and necessary, synthetic ones *a posteriori* and contingent; only the latter can give us any information about the world. Those, therefore, who have wished to maintain that there are certain facts that can be known to be true no matter what experience may bring, have been bound to argue that there may be propositions that are synthetic yet *a priori*. This position is opposed by empiricist philosophers, some of whom set up a criterion by which to separate propositions which were genuinely informative from those that were not; only when it was possible to indicate what observations would tend to verify and what to falsify a given proposition would it come into the former class. A proposition, the truth of which was compatible with any and every possible state of affairs, was vacuous; and, if its truth could not be said to follow from the meaning of its terms, to be discarded as a source of nothing but confusion and eyewash.

On its own ground this argument is irrefutable, since for the modern empiricist the impossibility of synthetic *a priori* propositions follows from the way in which he works out the usages of this family of terms. However, the importance of the distinction, though certainly very great, should still not be overrated; it may often be inappropriate, in particular when applied to propositions taken irrespective of context. Nevertheless, it remains a valuable tool of analysis for use whenever one needs to pin someone down— oneself included—to a clear and definite statement. Finally we noted that though there may be some qualms at calling analytic propositions (or statements), propositions at all, since they do not directly state anything, to do so will not matter provided that the situation is clear. I may add that I here propose to continue this usage as it is both current and convenient.

4

WHETHER VALUE JUDGMENTS[1] ARE STATEMENTS AND WHETHER VALUES ARE PROPERTIES

NOW that we have seen what sorts of things statements have generally been taken to be, we are in a position to consider more directly the question whether to say that something is good, is to make some kind of statement or not. What we can say so far is that if it is a statement of any kind, it must, on the traditional showing, always be open to clarification as either synthetic or analytic. So the thing to do must be to examine these two alternatives.

There have, in fact, been very few people who have taken seriously the suggestion that value judgments are analytic in the sense that I have tried to indicate. For one thing, such an interpretation must be unacceptable to those who hold that "the truth or falsity of moral judgments depends wholly on the nature of the objects which they are about". (See page 21.) On the contrary this might actually be one way of indicating the nature of synthetic propositions; the truth or falsity of an analytic proposition depends rather, as we know, on the meanings of the words out of which it is built. Moreover, it can hardly be said that an analytic proposition is about the nature of some object, for there is some difficulty as we have seen, in saying that it is about anything at all. For another thing, once the meanings of all the terms of an analytically true proposition are fully understood, there can be no further argument about its truth. This is only too clearly not the case as far as value judgments are concerned, nor do we try to convince those who do not

[1] At this stage I am taking it for granted that to say that something is good is normally to make a value judgment about it. See Chapter 5.

40

agree with us merely by explaining to them our own use of language. It would, if possible, be even more absurd to try to represent one's efforts to decide what one ought to do in some situation of awkward and unavoidable choice as arising out of puzzlement as to the proper use of English.

This general case seems as clear as can be. All the same it will be as well to consider by way of example an instance where it might still seem plausible to argue that a proposition expresses a value judgment and is yet analytic. Take the assertion "Murder is wrong". People sometimes argue that no-one could deny this who had properly understood the meaning of 'murder'; the counter assertion "murder is not always wrong" presents, so they say, a contradiction in terms, because if it was not wrong, it could not have been murder. If that is the case, certainly, it follows necessarily that if anything is murder, it is wrong and that this is an analytic proposition, its truth following from the way in which the term 'murder' is being used. But if it was not murder, what could it have been? The most likely answer, in one form or another, is that it was a case of justifiable killing, that is to say killing in self-defence or under extreme provocation or by accident and so on. The difference, in other words, between a case of justifiable killing and murder is simply that the latter is a case of unjustifiable killing. Once put like this, however, the situation becomes much clearer. The proposition "Unjustifiable killing is wrong" is true—analytically—because 'unjustifiable' and 'wrong' are both evaluative terms of very much the same type. Categorically to say, on the other hand, that *all killing* is wrong is to make a moral judgment, which can be and is disputed. It certainly cannot be established by reference to the meaning of the word 'killing', for there is nothing self-contradictory in the suggestion that killing is not in all circumstances wrong, even though you may hold that in fact it is.

The word 'murder', as normally used, seems then to contain two distinct elements, which we can find separated out in a phrase like 'unjustifiable killing' and which we

D   41

may call 'evaluative' and 'descriptive' respectively. The term 'descriptive' has, admittedly, certain drawbacks, but it is intended to indicate that the word 'killing', to take this particular example, is used to refer to the facts as neutrally and with as little element of evaluation as possible. (In any case, it is again one of those terms with which it is worth while being familiar in view of their frequent occurrence in the writings of modern philosophers.) There are a great number of words which perform this double function, but in any case where it seems that their use may lead to confusion, it should always be possible to separate out some non-evaluative way of alluding to the actual facts. An assertion such as "Murder is wrong" may be said to be analytic only because the same evaluation appears in both halves; it is like saying that wrong killing is wrong.

It is still just possible that somebody might argue that the proposition "Anything which is unjustifiable is wrong", which seems indisputably analytic, expresses a value judgment and an important one at that, since being completely general it applies not only to killing but to an indefinite number of other cases as well[1]. The main trouble with such an argument is that it seems that it would commit one to saying that the proposition "Anything which is wrong is wrong" expresses a value judgment too. This proposition very evidently says nothing about anything and, where nothing is being 'judged', it would seem very odd to say that a value judgment is being expressed. This, indeed, merely comes back to the fact that while analytic propositions are empty, value judgments, if they are anything at all, are something more than expressions exhibiting the ways in which different words are related to each other.

[1] It might, of course, be argued that the terms were recognised as belonging to two quite different contexts and that if the proposition were fully expressed, it might read "anything which is *legally* unjustifiable is *morally* wrong". To say this would admittedly be to say something substantial; but since it would at least be meaningful to assert the contrary, the proposition could in this case no longer be treated as analytic.

Suppose, for example, that when I say "murder is wrong" my assertion is to be taken as analytic. All it would tell you in such a case would be that whenever I refer to an instance of killing as murder, I consider the killing unjustifiable. If I do not consider it unjustifiable, I shall not use the word 'murder'. But while my assertion will have told you that I use the term 'murder' in this way always to express my disapproval, it will have done nothing at all to tell you of what sorts of killing I actually disapprove. It will have shown you what the word 'murder' means in my way of using it, but that is all; nothing is said about what sorts of things I actually disapprove and so no value judgment is made.

There is another well-known slogan to which it may be worth referring here; "An 'ought' can never be derived from an 'is' ". This originates in certain remarks by David Hume and is, incidentally, a frequent counter of exchange between teachers and students of philosophy in the commerce of lectures and exams. In the more sober and pompous terminology I have been introducing, it amounts to saying that no judgment of value can be analytically derived from a purely descriptive statement of fact. This, in its turn, it is interesting to note, amounts back to saying that no genuine value judgment can be analytic. For if we stick to our refusal to count expressions vacuously linking equivalent value terms as proper moral judgments, we must say that in any such judgment there will be at least two elements, an element by which reference is made to that which the judgment is about and the element of evaluation; and such a judgment could be said to be analytic only if the latter could be said to be involved in the meaning of the former[1] in the way in which 'being female' is involved in the meaning of 'mare'. It is this possibility that the slogan uncompromisingly rejects.

---

[1] By 'meaning' is to be understood, of course, the rules governing the intelligible use of a word or phrase and not, as is often colloquially the case, the general significance of whatever the term refers to.

Someone who has taken the last chapter very much to heart may want to know whether this slogan is itself analytic or synthetic. This raises another question of fundamental importance, for the distinction between evaluation and description underlies the whole of our argument. All will depend, therefore, on how we make the distinction and whether we suceed in doing it with sufficient clarity. This is so important a point that it calls for considerable discussion and we shall come back to it in Chapters 8 and 9. Meanwhile, however, I propose to risk taking your understanding of this difference for granted.

Our present situation is, then, that we cannot be satisfied with the suggestion that value judgments are analytic. The alternative possibility that they are embodied in synthetic propositions has been taken much more seriously by a great many different philosophers. The question can be tackled in two main different ways, one direct and the other indirect; and it will be best to start by taking the latter approach.

There has been a great deal of discussion, particularly in the last 50 years or so, about whether 'goodness' is some kind of property or not and if so, what kind. This word 'property' is an awkward term to handle like so many others which have a mixed tradition of partly technical, partly colloquial uses behind them. But we may perhaps avoid going into these technical associations for the present by saying simply that it has seemed most natural to many people to suppose that if a value judgment is a synthetic proposition about some object or event, its function can only be to ascribe to that object or event some characteristic or property. To say that pleasure is good is on this view to say that in so far as anything is pleasant it possesses the property (or quality) of goodness; to say that cruelty is wrong is to add something important to the (factual) description of a cruel act or person. This view has the advantages of being comparatively straight-forward and, above all, of providing an obvious sense for the claim that the truth of a value judgment rests on the nature of whatever it is about—in the same way as does the truth of any other assertion of fact.

The crucial question is, of course, how to decide whether any given word or phrase stands for a property or not. (This is very much the same question as how to decide whether or not a sentence is genuinely descriptive.) Perhaps the most helpful account is that according to which we are only allowed to talk of properties where we can envisage some procedure by which to decide whether a given object or event has the property. The two obvious types of procedure are direct observation on the one hand and some more or less indirect calculation or routine on the other. In any case of obstinate disagreement we have to try and establish whether our opponent has any sensory defect, whether he has misunderstood or misapplied the routine—he may, for example, have made a mistake in some mathematical calculation—or whether he is simply using the language in some different way from ourselves. To locate the source of trouble may in practice be exceedingly difficult, but once it is located, the disagreement should in principle be cleared up. In other words, if you and I disagree about whether something has a certain property or not, and if[1] we are using our words on the basis of the same standards of meaning, one of us must be wrong; there are, in these circumstances, no two ways about the facts.

At first sight this certainly does not seem to be the position as far as value judgments are concerned. Where matters of right and wrong are the subject of dispute, our disagreement may persist even though we may be content that we are both speaking the same language and agreed on all matters of observations and of calculation or routine. People have such irreducible disagreements over value judgments even when they both come from the same community. But there are, as is very well known, far greater

---

[1] This is, admittedly, a very big 'if', behind which may lurk a great variety of problems.

chances of disagreement over really serious issues if we come from different communities or backgrounds. The question that confronts anyone who wants to maintain in this situation that values are properties, is whether it might after all always be possible to envisage some procedure to settle such disagreements and whether, whatever the disputants might think, the sources of disagreement must always lie in some discrepancy of observation, calculation, or both.

We should try to see very briefly what sort of suggestions might be made in support of such a position. As far as observation is concerned, it would hardly be maintained that values could directly be seen or tasted, touched, heard or smelt; the thesis has nearly always been that their presence could be detected only by some special moral or aesthetic sense or perhaps by intuition or even by reason itself. But, it seems natural to ask, if men do have these special senses or intuitions, this surely makes their stubborn disagreements about values even more puzzling? After all, there are no parallel disagreements about the ordinary material characteristics of things between people with the five normal physical senses.

One of the two main lines along which it is common to meet this objection is to accept that there is often hesitation and disagreement in the recognition of values, but to maintain that this is something that must be learnt by practice as well as by precept, and that not only individuals but also whole communities, and even maybe mankind itself, have to go through the process of education. As rough and ready examples, the cases of the wine connoisseur and the art critic are often quoted, for both of them have to go through a long period of apprenticeship and training. The other main possibility is to argue that on basic issues there is after all far more agreement than disagreement. Incest taboos are often taken as a supporting example, for incest, one is told, is regarded as wrong by even the most primitive of tribes. Another argument that is frequently used in support of this point is that though different peoples may disagree on the secondary question as to which sorts of conduct are wrong and which are right, they are all agreed on the fundamental issue that there is a distinction between right and wrong conduct to be made. Finally it is possible to appeal to the familiar distinction between ends and means. Everyone recognises that one may praise something as a means to some end without committing oneself to any evaluation of that end considered in itself; and furthermore that what may be the best means to an end in one context may be quite inappropriate as a means to that end in another. So many philosophers have wanted to explain the great variety of things that people call 'good' by saying that nearly always these are cases of something or other being commended as a means. There are many possible ends and even more possible means; but, so this argument runs, there are underneath this variety only very few ends which themselves possess the property of goodness and which are generally recognised to do so.

If we accepted this last argument, then we might very plausibly account for disagreements over value judgments as being due to disagreements less of observation than of calculation. For among the ends which have been suggested as the bases for all secondary value judgments are, to take perhaps the three best known examples, 'pleasure', 'the greatest happiness of the greatest number' and 'anything whose existence or occurrence is in accordance with the will of God'. But obviously there can be enormous difficulties in the way of calculating which of two incompatible actions will, if chosen, have the consequences that lead in the long run to the greatest happiness of the greatest number; or of deciding between rival theological arguments as to what is or is not in accordance with God's will. So taking all these arguments together it might be suggested that there is in fact very little disagreement among people who have the necessary experience and wisdom as to the few very general aims that underlie our conduct, but that over the attainment of these aims there is room for much genuine disagreement.

There are, needless to say, a great many things that can be and have been said against these sorts of suggestions. We must mention a few of them here, though unsystematically and without going into detail; for it will not be worth our while to get really involved in the complicated controversies that take place around these particular points. Briefly then, there is, in the first place, no complete agreement about the universality of even such beliefs as the wrongness of incest. In any case, it is often added, there are perfectly good psychological or sociological explanations for its being generally disapproved of and so no need to postulate mysterious faculties for the observation of elusive properties for neither of which there is any independent evidence. Secondly, the analogies of the wine connoisseur and the art critic are both very misleading. Whether or not the aim of the art critic is to pick out certain specific aesthetic properties is highly disputable and, in any case, one of the very points at issue. While as for wine, to be able to discriminate the date and origin of different vintages is one thing and to range them in order of merit very much another; it is far from obvious that the second involves the discovery of any further properties to those which may have been relevant to the first. Thirdly, quite apart from the difficulties of calculating all the consequences of an action if we should want to do so, in many cases of moral decision we do not in fact go in for calculating at all, but rather take our stand, choosing to damn the consequences. Fourthly, to say that everyone makes a distinction between right and wrong is, even if true, to say no more than that everybody has preferences. Fifthly, and more positively, there is an old and very respectable thesis that to learn the nature of morals is to learn how to behave in society and has nothing to do with the development of a highly refined power of observation.

None of these counter arguments, of course, actually

prove that values are not properties of objects or events. They attempt rather to show how little reason there is for talking of properties in this context and to bring out some of the difficulties that will be involved in doing so. In fact some people, who have wished to cling at all costs to the view that values are properties, have nevertheless been so impressed by these difficulties that they have tried to construe value judgments as statements about the speaker's reactions; e.g. "This object has the property of being approved of by me", which would not exclude the possibility of its having at the same time the property of 'being disapproved of by you'. It would now generally be admitted that this is a most implausible suggestion. For one thing when we disagree with other people's value judgments, we do not dispute them on the grounds that they are lying or mistaken about what they really approve of. In any case, a theory which dealt in such unlikely properties as 'being disapproved of by you' might retain the original banner, but none of the positions over which the banner was originally waved. If we cannot say that values are properties of the events and objects that we are interested in, we might as well accept the position that they are best not called 'properties' at all.

In my view, this is indeed the best solution. But I doubt whether the arguments I have so far put forward would clinch the matter for anyone who was not already convinced on other grounds. There is, we must admit, a certain looseness in suggesting that we should be "only allowed to talk of properties where we can envisage some procedure by which to decide whether a given object or event has a property or not". (See page 45.) Quite apart from many statements about the far distant past, to test the truth of which there is no procedure that we can envisage, it may often happen that an assertion of which one generation can think of no means of testing is submitted by the next to empirical test. In such cases what matters cannot be whether or not we are at any given moment able to think of some procedure by which a statement might in practice be tested, but whether we can say what would be or would have been different if certain observations could be or could have been made. Here, however, we come back to the general situation regarding synthetic propositions for the last remark could have come straight out of the discussion in the previous chapter. It is time, therefore, to take up this question directly.

You will remember from the last chapter that all synthetic propositions are by their very nature *a posteriori;* that is to say that their truth or falsity depends ultimately on the results of observation, on the nature of the facts which the propositions are 'about'. But if we try to talk now of value judgments as *a posteriori*, we shall get some surprising results. For to say that the truth or falsity of a statement depends upon the nature of the facts is to say that it is, in principle at any rate, liable to be upset by their observation. But what possible observation could count as evidence against the assertion that killing for its own sake is wrong? To go on looking out for an instance of killing for its own sake that might prove an exception to this rule is no more sensible than watching a cricket match for the man who might score nought without making a duck. (The case would be just the same, of course, with the assertion that killing for its own sake is right. Whatever else one might do, it would be pointless simply to insist that someone who thought like this should try and observe great numbers of such killings in the hope that he might eventually spot one that was wrong.) In the same way, whatever the considerations by which a value judgment may be supported, it would be senseless to aim at confirming it by carrying out experiments. There can be no waiting to see if the next instance of killing for its own sake is wrong; we know in advance that it must be[1]. Future observations may conceivably upset the most firmly established beliefs as to matters of fact; (the suggestion is not, that is to say,

[1] Or not, as the case may be, according to the principles we hold.

logically self-contradictory). But if aimless cruelty is thought to be wrong, it does not make sense to suggest that some possible future observation may disclose an instance of aimless cruelty that is right.

There are three classes of what may seem to be exceptions to what I have just said and so I had better say a word about each. In the first place, one may approve or disapprove of something because one has not fully realised either what it is itself really like or what its consequences are going to be. For example, some people who approve of capital punishment as a deterrent would no longer do so if it were possible to convince them that it did not have this effect; and others who have at a distance approved of warfare (perhaps as the proper field for the exercise of manly qualities), have no longer approved of it after seeing it at close quarters. What experience has shown here, however, is that the original value judgment was based on a mistaken or inadequate view of the facts. Moreover, the facts, once discovered, do not *compel* one to change one's mind in the same way as the facts about pillar boxes in France would *compel* anyone to retract who had previously asserted that all pillar boxes in Europe were red. I was not, in the last paragraph, trying to make the absurd suggestion that value judgments are totally independent of facts, but that they are not totally dependent upon them either and that once the facts are satisfactorily ascertained there is no sense in awaiting further instances of the same sort to see if the same value judgment is appropriate.

The second type of exception involves a somewhat similar point. There are times when we cannot avoid a clash of principles, the subordination of one moral principle to another. Someone might, for example, believe both that one ought always to keep promises and that one should always place the preservation of other people's lives above all other considerations; and quite honestly never have thought of the possibility that these two principles could on occasion clash, until the facts placed him in just such an unpleasant situation. In such a case there is indeed a sense in which it is the observation of these facts that compels a revision of a moral principle, but again it is not of the same sort as where the facts compel a revision of some factual statement. An ordinary empirical synthetic proposition is in principle open to falsification because it must exclude, if it is true, some state of affairs, and it is impossible to guarantee except on the basis of observation that such a state of affairs has not or will not turn up. A moral principle, on the other hand, such as "promise breaking is wrong", is in itself incompatible with no series of observations; what it may in certain circumstances be incompatible with are other moral principles. Mere observation of these circumstances, however, cannot determine which of the two principles should take precedence. Facts may be such as logically to compel the abandonment of an empirical assertion, but while the discovery that two moral principles can clash may arise from the discovery of certain matters of fact and these may compel the relaxation of *one* of the principles, they cannot dictate which of the two it shall be. In other words, the 'truth' of a value judgment remains entirely independent of any possible factual observations taken on their own. In any case, though a general principle may seem to admit to exceptions, we could always say, if we wanted to, that that was because it was over generally expressed. Thus it is possible, and perhaps better to say not that the facts have disclosed an exception to our principle but that they have compelled us to recast it in a somewhat restricted form. What we may now say is that it is wrong to break promises in situations of a certain type (when, for example, the preservation of other people's lives is clearly not at stake); but if in any given situation to break a promise would be wrong, we are bound to say that this holds true for all other situations of exactly the same sort. To this there can be no exception whatsoever.

Thirdly, it is often suggested that principles which may be valid for one sort of community at one period of time may be quite inappropriate for another community at a different period of time; for example, that given the circumstances, way of life and aspirations of a community, the principle of the sanctity of human life may be valid for that community but quite irrelevant to the way of life of another community in different circumstances and with different aspirations. From this 'relativist' point of view, it would perhaps make sense to suggest that though aimless cruelty does not at present fit in with the accepted forms of social life, it might fit in with some other form of society; and on this basis the assertion that such cruelty is wrong, might turn out to be concerned with matters of fact about a particular form of society. Another interpretation might be that in the present circumstances, aimless cruelty stands in the way of some general social end such as the harmony of interests of the community at large, whereas in other circumstances it might advance this end; on this basis the assertion would be concerned with the factual relationships of means to ends. But either way it is only turned into a synthetic proposition by no longer treating it as a value judgment; except in so far as the speaker considers the harmony of interests in a community as an end right and proper in itself, beyond the relativist shifts to which any means to that end may be subject—and therefore outside this third relativist class of exceptions.

Finally, exceptions apart, what of an outright denial of my argument that value judgments are not open to falsification by experience in the same straight-forward manner as ordinary factual statements? Could one not say that aimless cruelty might at one time have the property of wrongness and at another time not, just as pillar boxes are sometimes but not always red? Using this curious language of 'having' and 'not having properties', the suggestion may for a moment, seem feasible. But consider a sentence like "these two actions are to all intents and purposes, of exactly the same type, but one is right and the other wrong". This surely is an impossible sentence. It may be that the assertion that aimless cruelty is wrong, is over general and that it would be safer to specify it more closely; we might talk of 'aimless cruelty in certain sorts of situations'. But however we specify the action we are interested in condemning, one can surely not at the same time admit the possibility of another action just like it in the relevant ways being this time not wrong but right. (Indeed we have already made substantially the same point two paragraphs back.)

The fact that value judgments seem to be universal in this way and that there is something absurd in the suggestion that they may be *a posteriori* or contingent on what is observed to be the case has, then, led many philosophers, anxious to maintain that they provide genuinely factual information, to claim that they are not only synthetic but also *a priori*. Synthetic because they are about the world; but *a priori* because they are in an important sense independent of it. We have only to refer back to the previous chapter to see how this claim must have appeared to those engaged in setting up a criterion by which to recognise genuine empirical statements. Not only did it seem to be wrong, but it presented a challenge to the very basis of their philosophy. (Remember that there only had to be one case of a synthetic *a priori* proposition for their whole system to be discredited.) Their reaction to this challenge was firm to the point of eccentricity. If value judgments are neither analytic nor *a posteriori*, they said, then the propositions in which they appear to be embodied are not genuine propositions at all; they are but pseudo-propositions to be regarded as meaningless or nonsense.

This over-emphatic and paradoxical way of putting the position, has had certain unfortunate consequences. If we accept that any statement must be capable of being clarified as either analytic or synthetic and, at the same time, that value judgments cannot fall into either of these categories, then it follows quite simply that a value judgment cannot be counted as a kind of statement. This, as we must shortly recall, is a conclusion that not everyone has been able to accept with comfort. But to say that any utterance which is neither a statement of fact nor, perhaps, expresses an analytic proposition, must on that account be meaningless, is not only calculated to shock but is also patently false. (That is, of course, if the word 'meaningless' is to be taken in any normal sense and not as a technical term simply equivalent to 'neither an analytic nor a synthetic proposition'.) As a result, the real nature of the situation has been obscured and often misrepresented, and the need for a new type of analysis lost in the dust of charges of moral irresponsibility. Actually, the 'verificationists', agreeing rapidly that some kinds of nonsense were more important than others, did try to produce some alternative accounts of the function of moral judgments. They are in part, it was said, like exclamations evincing favour or disfavour, such, for instance, as 'Boo!' or 'Hurrah!'; and in part like imperatives bidding other people to adopt similar attitudes. This is not the best moment to discuss the various objections that have been made to the implausibilities of this doctrine and the elaborations attempted in order that these objections might be met. But in all this, it is interesting to note, it was generally assumed that logic dealt only with the two kinds of statement and that the study of value judgments must accordingly fall outside the logical field. This goes a good way to accounting for the comparative lack of interest taken in them by these philosophers. The main point to retain, however, is that the fact that value judgments seem to be neither analytic nor synthetic leads to the conclusion that they cannot be classified as statements; and thence, of course, to some puzzle as to the sense in which they may be true or false.

There is one further important point to be added. Once again I would not claim that the arguments I have so far put forward actually prove that value judgments are not embodied in synthetic propositions. The effect of my arguments is cumulative but even so, if one is sufficiently ingenious, one may still produce enough counter-suggestions to fight further delaying actions. So suppose for a moment that we allow that 'goodness' is the name of some sort of property and that a judgment such as "kindness and tolerance are good" presents a synthetic proposition. What then becomes of the distinction between evaluation and description and of the slogan that "an 'ought' can never be derived from an 'is' "? For surely to ascribe a property to something is to describe that thing as being of a certain sort. When I discover that water has the property of being a conductor of electricity I am adding to what is known about water, to the ways in which it may be accurately described. But a pure description of the facts should in principle be neutral, implying nothing about what ought to be done and leaving it an open question as to whether one should approve or disapprove of the state of affairs that has been described. "If that is how things are, that is how they are", we might say, "but that in itself does not make me approve of them". To say that something is good is, however, precisely to commit oneself to approval; to say that it is right to a view as to what ought to be done. At least this is so if the dictionary is right in its view that 'good' is 'the most general term of commendation in the English language'. If, in spite of this, it is insisted that goodness is a property and that to call anything good is essentially to offer descriptive information about it, we shall need some other means of commending things once described. We cannot have it both ways at once. In this way the recognition of this distinction between what I have called—not wholly satisfactorily—evaluation and description is fundamental to the whole argument.

The detail of this chapter has been somewhat intricate, but the main points should be clear. It would be difficult and implausible, it turns out, to treat genuine value judgments as either analytic or synthetic. They cannot, therefore, be statements if we take the term together with this traditional classification. Thus our preliminary question is answered. This brings us back to the problem of more obvious interest as to the sense, if any, in which they may be said to be true or false. The majority of those who have wanted to say that they can be true or false in what seems a straight-forward objective sense have thought that a value must be some kind of property. The difficulties in the way of holding this view are, we have seen, part and parcel of the difficulties in the way of holding that value judgments are synthetic propositions; and it meets in the last resort with the fundamental objection that it is incompatible with the recognition of the distinction between description and evaluation. The nature of this distinction is the most important of a number of points raised in this chapter which will turn up again later on.

5

THE MEANING OF 'GOOD'

THE main argument of the last chapter was to the general
effect that value judgments can be treated neither as synthetic
nor analytic and therefore cannot be treated as statements.
At once one wants to ask, if they are not statements, what
are they? It is obviously silly to say that if they are not
statements, then they are nothing meaningful at all and, as
I have already said, the early empiricist view that this was
the case lasted only a very short time—if, indeed, it had ever
been meant to be taken literally at all. It will be no more
possible in this chapter than it was in the last to try to follow
the recent history of moral philosophy, from the time of
these extremist theories up to the present day. Instead I
shall try to put forward the outline of one alternative view
that has been very much discussed in the last few years. I
shall not be trying to give an exposition of the views of any
particular philosopher; but my account is certainly very
much influenced by the views of Mr. R. M. Hare[1], whose
work in moral philosophy has been at least as important as
that of anyone else in recent times.

We may start from the simple fact about typical value
judgments upon which we have already twice remarked
towards the end of the last chapter. This is that while it
makes sense to say of any two objects that they are the same
in every respect except one, namely that one is red and the
other is not, it does not make sense to say of any two
objects they are exactly the same with the single exception

[1] See especially his book '*The Language of Morals*'. Mr. Hare has, of
course, no responsibility whatsoever for the simplified and perhaps
garbled use that I may make of some of his ideas.

that only one of them is good. This is because while the use of a term like 'red' is sufficient to mark a factual difference between any two objects (or events etc.), the use of a term like 'good' is not. If someone tells us that he has painted two pictures only one of which is good, we are naturally led to ask him what is the difference between them. Suppose he replied "that just is the difference, one is good and the other is not"; most people would find this quite unintelligible. We can only understand the different evaluations that he gives to these two pictures on the assumption that they are based on some factual difference between them, a factual difference that may provide the reason—good or bad as the case may be, for we are not bound to accept it—for the differing evaluations. If there is no factual difference, there is no basis for a differing evaluation.

The fact that the *primary* use of the word 'good' is not a descriptive one, that is to say that it is not *primarily* used to point to any factual characteristics of the object or event that is judged to be 'good', is perhaps most clearly shown by considering, as we have just done, a case where two objects are explicitly compared. But even when there is no explicit comparison involved, the primary use of 'good' is still non-descriptive. One way of showing this is as follows. Suppose you overhear me saying that something is good without knowing what sort of thing I am talking about. The fact that you have heard me say this will tell you nothing whatsoever about the sort of thing it is and, since in the nature of the case you cannot know from what point of view I am speaking, you would have nothing to go on to help you to recognise the object in question. Compare the situation where you overhear me saying that something is red. Obviously this is very far from being a complete description of anything, but it does at least convey some factual or descriptive information. For one thing you would be able to say quite definitely of anything that was not red, that I had not been talking about it. But this does not mean that when you hear me calling something good you do not understand the meaning of what I am saying. On the contrary, you would understand perfectly well that I was rating something or other comparatively highly, even though you would not know what I was commending or why I was commending it in this way. Thus even in a context where no factual information whatsover is conveyed, 'good' still has its clear commendatory meaning.

We may find it helpful here to refer to a distinction that Hare makes, with this sort of situation in mind, between meaning and criteria. The *meaning* of a term like 'good' lies in its evaluatory or commendatory function; the *criteria* are the factual characteristics to which one would be bound, if challenged, to refer in support of an evaluation. For example, when I tell you that there is a very good film on at the local cinema this week, I indicate to you my approval of the film[1]; if I go on to explain to you explicitly just what sort of a film it is, I then give you the criteria on which I based my view that the film was a good one. My criteria for good films may, of course, be different from the next man's, and even in my own case my criteria for films are obviously totally different both from my criteria for good meals and my criteria for good social behaviour. Thus in this sense of the word 'meaning', 'good' means the same thing when I apply it, to refer back to the example of Chapter 2, either to cider or to arguments; it is the criteria that differ in the two cases.

If in any context you know the basis on which my evaluation is made, if, that is to say, you know what are the

[1] Notice that to indicate my approval is not the same thing as to state that I approve. This may seem a pedantic distinction, but you will remember that in the last chapter we referred to the absurd view that value judgments are some sort of statements about the speaker; and in calling this view absurd there was no exaggeration. Any argument about the truth of a statement can only take place by reference to what the statement is about. But, as we have said, we do not argue about value judgments as if they were statements about the speaker. If 'statement' is one of the key words in our argument, we must obviously be very careful about how we use other words belonging to the same family, like, for example, the verb 'to state'.

sort of criteria on which I usually base that sort of evaluation in that sort of context, then certainly my evaluation will convey factual information too. If you happen to know what sort of films I approve of, then in telling you that I approve of a film I shall in effect be telling you something about what sort of film it is, even though that is not the explicit point of my remark. Of course the converse is also true; if I tell you explicitly what sort of film it is, then if you are familiar with my standards in this context, I shall have indicated by my description, without expressing it directly, whether I approve of it or not. There are, as we have already noted in Chapter 4, many primarily descriptive words which, because certain standards are widely recognised, regularly convey certain evaluative information; a word like 'cheat' is normally used both to describe and to disapprove at the same time. There is never a completely clear cut border between value terms and descriptive terms. As Hare points out, when standards become very rigid and a matter of strict social convention, then words which were once value terms may effectively turn into terms with a primarily descriptive function. Hare discusses the example of an Indian Army officer for whom the term 'good man' is simply a shorthand way of describing somebody as a capable polo player, an enthusiastic sticker of pigs and certain other similar things. Anyone new coming into this sort of community might accept their language, and in particular their sort of use of the phrase 'good man', without always intending or even being understood to to intend to show thereby his approval either of capable polo players or of enthusiastic pig stickers. Indeed this sort of community may easily change in such a way that hardly anybody, except the oldest members, continues to approve of people on these particular grounds, while yet everyone goes on with the habit of using the term 'good man' in the same descriptive way. In some curious cases a value term may first become conventionalised into a descriptive term and then through a change of standards, either general or with reference to a particular context, actually take on the opposite evaluative significance from that which it originally had; a very good example of this is the way in which some children may scornfully describe others as 'goody-goodies'. But in spite of this, the primary function or meaning of 'good' remains that of evaluating or, more specifically, that of commending; nobody would be called a 'goody-goody' if his behaviour was not of a type that a certain class of grown-ups could normally be expected to commend.

Naturally, if we use the word 'meaning' simply in this way, we are to some extent imposing a stipulative definition upon it. The very fact that many people say that 'good' means something quite different when applied to cider from what it does when applied to arguments, is enough to show that there is in ordinary language a sense of the word 'meaning' in which they are right. Ordinary language is after all nothing more or less than the language which ordinary people speak. All the same, we shall be justified in stipulating a somewhat more restricted use for a term like 'meaning' if as a result of doing so we find ourselves in a better position to avoid puzzles and muddles. If 'good' really did mean something totally different in each different context, then it is hard to see how people could learn to use it so freely throughout the innumerable variety of contexts in which they do use it. And anyhow perhaps the best justification for making the distinction between criteria and meaning in this way of Hare's is that once it is put to us in this way, it seems perfectly natural and right. 'Good' is, as the dictionary says, simply, primarily and in the great majority of contexts, the most general term of commendation that we have. It is surely appropriate that this should be called its 'meaning'.

Here, then, and provided that we are prepared to accept this interpretation of the word 'meaning', is the answer to the question with which we started, "what does it mean to say of anything that it is good"? It is that to say that it is good is to commend it. But in taking this long way round to the answer that is to be found in the dictionary, one thing has become clear that we might well have overlooked had we gone straight to the dictionary in the first place. This is that to commend something is not to describe it; to say that kindness is good is to state no sort of fact (it is to make no sort of statement); it is to commend kindness. So, remembering the close family relationships that exist between such terms as 'statement', 'fact' and 'true', we have given much sharper point to the question whether there is any sense in which commendations may be said to be true or false. This question we shall at last tackle directly in the next chapter.

Before going on to that, however, there are two or three other points that we had better mention here. First there is one of the many loose ends that may as well be gathered up now. Many people tend to say, as I mentioned in Chapter 2, that the meaning of the word 'good' is quite exceptionally vague. If we understand the term 'meaning' in the way suggested by Hare, this suggestion seems to be quite unjustified. Of course, the meaning of 'good' is vague to some extent; but then this is true of almost all words in ordinary speech. The word 'red', for example, is vague to very much the same extent; there are after all many borderline cases of colours, where we should be hard put to it to decide whether or not to call the colour in question 'red'. But there is nothing strange or particularly inconvenient about this, and though we can never eliminate vagueness of this sort altogether, we can, if we wish, introduce a much more precise range of colour terms for our special purposes as carpet dealer[1] or paint manufacturer as the case may be. The same is true of the word 'good'; if we want to introduce a range of terms enabling us to make a series of more finely graduated evaluations, it is always possible to do so. Presumably people who have suggested that 'good' is quite exceptional in its vagueness have given all their attention to the unlimited possible variety of criteria and so taken them to be the meaning; anyone who does this will naturally be

[1] See Professor Stephen Toulmin's *'The Place of Reason in Ethics'*, page 12.

unable to find anything in common between all the different sets of criteria of which he might be able to think and, finding that they have nothing in common, will be inclined in a baffled sort of way to identify that nothing with the meaning of 'good'.

In the second place there is a point which has already been mentioned in this chapter, but which I have probably not sufficiently emphasised. "The meaning of a term like 'good' lies", we said, "in its evaluatory or commendatory function; the criteria are the factual characteristics to which one would be bound, if challenged, to refer in support of an evaluation". That is to say that these factual characteristics are the initial reasons that one would have to give to justify the evaluation one had made. This reappearance of the word 'reason' is worth noting. Of course, we are very far here from the view that value judgments are made by Reason understood as a special sort of faculty—whatever exactly that might mean. But there is something in this repeated insistence on the rational nature of value judgments. For, as we have just seen, anyone who makes different evaluations of two similar objects or events must find reasons for the distinction he makes in some factual difference between them. In the same way, even where no obvious comparison is involved it is always appropriate to insist that someone who has said that something is good, should provide his reasons for having said so; that is that he should say clearly what were the factual characteristics which served him in this context as criteria for his evaluation. So there is one definite sense at any rate in which value judgments may be said to be rational; it is always proper to demand reasons for them.

This leads on to the difficult question of the difference between saying that something is good on the one hand and on the other saying simply that one likes it. It might well be said that it is equally appropriate to ask anyone who has said that he likes something what are his reasons for doing so. And so in a way it is. The difference is that in this case it is not always appropriate to insist. Suppose that I say that I like Mr. Brown and you ask me why. I may very naturally and quite intelligibly reply "There is no particular reason; I just like him, that is all". Here there may be no use in your insisting that I must have a reason; I can fairly go on replying that I simply feel like that and that is all there is to the matter. I cannot, however, just dig in my toes in this way if I had started by saying not that I liked him, but that Brown was a good man. To your question "Why is he a good man, what is there good about him?", "He just is so" is not a possible answer, not possible because as it stands it is not fully intelligible. In this instance you are perfectly entitled to insist.

Suppose, to push the matter a bit further, that you do insist, when I have said that somebody is good, on knowing why and that I am in fact unable to produce any reasons. In practice this alone would not make my assertion unintelligible. For one thing I might be prepared to accept that it could quite fairly be translated into an expression of simple liking. The word 'good' certainly is very often used in this way, though quite how often is impossible to say since in most cases the question is never explicitly raised. Another possibility is that I might reply that though I had not yet thought about the matter sufficiently to make my reasons clear even to myself, I was quite sure that there were some and that if I thought about the matter enough I should be able to find them. Even mathematicians may with experience find that they are able to arrive at the correct solution by a sort of intuitive leap before having traced out the steps by which the solution may be established; (it may indeed sometimes be a very long time before the mathematician can prove that his solution is correct, even though he feels perfectly sure that it is so).

These two different ways by which I might reply to your insistent demand for my reasons for an evaluation both raise further problems of their own. It would be silly and unrealistic to expect people always to be prepared in advance to give clear and explicit reasons for their value judgments.

Yet obviously my reply that my reasons are just on the tip of my tongue but no further can, if repeated too often, become merely evasive. There can be no hard and fast rules about this. How far we trust a man's judgment must depend on circumstances, our knowledge of the man in question and on our own familiarity with the subject matter. At any rate provided I am willing to look for reasons for my value judgment, and at the same time to consider possible counter-reasons against it, I can justifiably maintain that it is a value judgment and not a mere expression of liking; though this claim is bound to become less and less plausible as time goes on and no evidence is produced.

The border line between liking somebody and valuing him highly is, though not always, nevertheless often a thin and shaky one; but the fact that it is difficult to locate it exactly means neither that it does not exist nor that it does not matter on which side of the border one may be. If I say that I like Mr. Brown, that is a fact about me. If I say that Brown is a good man and am prepared to support this with reasons, then I claim to say something that will hold good not only for Brown himself but for all others like him in the relevant ways, ways that are referred to in the reasons that I give. At the same time I suggest, what can quite well be the case, that my approval of Brown is wholly independent of my personal feelings of like or dislike towards him, and in this way I claim much more serious attention from other people than I should by a mere expression of private personal feeling. On the other hand, there is a price to be paid for this added impressiveness; a case supported by reasons is much more open to attack and possible defeat than is a mere stubborn assertion of personal feeling. In practice, of course, motives are often inextricably mixed. But even when the word 'good' is admittedly used as a simple expression of liking, there remains an interesting distinction between the sentences "I like X" and "X is good", a distinction that is marked by the use of the phrase 'expression of liking'. For the sentence "I like him" can obviously be treated as an assertion or statement of some sort about the speaker. I have already tried to provide some very brief explanation of the importance of distinguishing between expressions of liking and statements of liking for the sake of discussions such as the present one. Here there is the further difference that the *statement* "I like him" focuses attention on the speaker and, if we can put it this way, the purely personal nature of his liking. The *expression* "He is a good man", on the other hand, not only does not direct attention to the speaker, since it is not about him, but rather focuses attention on the object in the way in which a value judgment normally would. It does this because even when the word 'good' is used as a simple expression of liking, it retains some echo of its normal evaluative suggestion that there are reasons to be given for the judgment that are connected with the nature of whatever it is that the judgment is about.

We need to be a little careful if we are not to tie ourselves in knots over this distinction between statement and expression. It is a useful device to mark the difference between making on the one hand an *assertion about something* that might be true or false and, on the other, the verbal evincing of *feelings towards something*, which can be no more true or false than my action in biting my thumb. But, of course, it might very well be said that the most straight-forward way in which I can express my liking of somebody is simply to say that I like him; my statement is, that is to say, at the same time an expression of my liking. This may seem confusing, but the fact is that any utterance may perform more than one function or may be treated in more than one way at the same time. In some circumstances an assertion to the effect that I dislike Brown may be a most effective way of expressing my liking for him, if, for instance, I speak in such a way as to make it clear that the assertion is not only false but absurdly so. In the case of a positive assertion "I like him". we can say that the sentence functions both as a statement and as an expression of liking at the same time; though of

67

course this is a distinction that is only worth insisting on in the context of a semi-technical discussion such as the present one.

It should be pointed out, too, that the drift of this discussion has been towards stipulating a semi-technical usage for the term 'value judgment'. When we say that my assertion that Brown is a good man can only be treated as a value judgment provided that I am at least 'willing to look for reasons for my value judgment' (page 66), we may justify our saying so with the simple and conclusive reason that this is the way in which we decide to use the term 'value judgment'. However, this decision is not an arbitrary one. It is in pretty close accord with traditional ways of using the term and will be fully justified if it helps to make a little clearer the complexity of the ways in which we shift, for the most part unknowingly, from one position to another in ordinary thought and speech.

Finally, we should mention the very common use of sentences like "Brown is a good man" to quote value judgments that are in accord with generally accepted standards. In many ways this is like the purely descriptive use of the phrase 'good chap' simply as a shorthand form of 'capable polo player and enthusiastic pig sticker etc.'. In both cases the speaker's use of the commendatory expression is based on standards that either once were or now are accepted by other people, influential by virtue of rank or numbers or both. In neither case does the speaker commit himself by the use of the word 'good' to any personal approval. One might express the difference by saying that the full descriptive use of an expression like 'good chap' is an extreme or degenerate case of quoting an established judgment. In a way somebody's standards are being quoted, but for purely descriptive purposes. This sort of case is, I should imagine, in fact exceptionally rare. *Would* it have made sense even to the imaginary Indian Army officer to have described two subalterns as similar, as far as the qualities in which he was interested were concerned, except only that one was a good chap and the other was not? It might have done; but I am somewhat inclined to doubt it. At any rate it is much more common for value judgments to be quoted as an actor might speak them in a play, quoted, that is to say, without the speaker intending thereby to accept personal responsibility for them, but quoted nevertheless as value judgments rather than used for purely descriptive purposes.

Moreover, there is a further and important point to be mentioned in this connection. Up to now I have been talking of value judgments as if they were essentially matters of individual personal responsibility and as if the use of the word 'good' in a genuine value judgment was always to express the speakers' own individual commendation. This is certainly an assumption that is made by most philosophers who have discussed this subject recently; but it is not one that should be allowed to pass unnoticed. We cannot in fact attempt to discuss it now; but I mention it so that it shall not escape our attention, and also because it is worth making at this stage the point that most of us would actually be hard put to say of most of our value judgments whether they are our own or simply the quoted opinions of the community in which we live. The distinction is in fact so comparatively rarely applicable as to demand much further consideration.

To sum up then. The main argument of this chapter rests, it would be fair to say, on the distinction, borrowed from Mr. Hare, between meaning and criteria; and on the basis of this distinction we have been able to give a clear sense to the dictionary view that the meaning of 'good' lies in its commendatory function. It is certainly true that to say that something is good may often convey factual information, but this we have seen to be incidental to the main purpose for which the word is used. Moreover, a judgment to the effect that something is good must always be based on some factual characteristics of the thing in question, characteristics that provide reasons for any attempted justification of the judgment. Although the primary use of the word 'good' is this evaluatory or commendatory one, one will of course come across many others; and in particular we looked at some of the differences and similarities between saying "X is good" on the one hand and simply "I like X" on the other.

6

THE MEANING OF 'TRUE'

AFTER much apparently roundabout discussion, we have now settled on a reasonably straight-forward answer to the question of what it means to say that something is good. In this chapter we have left ourselves with the question of what it might mean to say that such an assertion was true. To answer this we now have to try and sort out some of the main ways in which this word 'true' is used. It is, in fact, like 'good' in a number of ways. It is a simple word used frequently by nearly everybody and used, in the ordinary way of things, without giving rise to difficulties or to misunderstandings; it is a word whose meaning people find strangely difficult to make explicit; it has, too, been the centre of many celebrated philosophic enquiries. We have seen that one of the most characteristic features of the word 'good' is that it is impossible to distinguish between any two things no matter what they may be, simply on the grounds that one of them is good while the other is not. This is yet another and more important point that the words 'good' and 'true' have in common. Inevitably, though, the matter is not quite straight-forward and needs looking at with some care.

Suppose we ask, then, whether two statements can be exactly the same as each other except only that while one is true the other is not. This is not altogether an easy question to answer at first sight. The main difficulty is, as I have said in Chapter 3, that one can not think of a statement "as something which has some sort of independent existence and whose nature can be determined . . . without reference to any particular context". Suppose, for example, that you and I both say "I am hungry". In a way we are certainly saying the same thing. Yet it could easily be the case that your assertion is true and mine false or vice versa. Or suppose

71

again that I think it to be polite always to say after my lunch "Well, I enjoyed that". Almost certainly my assertion will be less strictly true on some days than others, though again I can in a perfectly natural sense be accused of saying the same thing every day. In the first case the two utterances of the sentence "I am hungry" referred to different people; in the second my daily assertion "I enjoyed that", refers each time to a different meal. Many people have thought that the best way of describing situations like this where the same sentence is used to refer to different things or occasions, is to say that the same *sentence* is used to make different *statements;* in this way a semi-technical distinction is introduced between the terms 'statement' and 'sentence'. Certainly we need to make some such distinction if we are to have any hope of talking about one statement being the same as another without falling at once into quite unmanageable muddles.

At any rate if we do use the term 'statement' in some such way as this—and this is yet another matter that turns out to be full of complications once one goes into it thoroughly—it seems reasonably clear that there would at the very least be something unusual and odd in talking of two statements differing from each other only in that while one was true the other was false. This suggests, if we follow the analogy of 'good', that to say that a statement is true is not, whatever else it may be, to describe it as having certain factual characteristics; (for example, the factual characteristic of corresponding to some other and, in most cases, non-linguistic fact). But if this is what one is not doing, how in fact is one using the word 'true'? In the case of 'good' our general answer was that the term is, primarily anyhow, used in order to commend. No such general answer seems to be so immediately obvious in the case of 'true', but some people at any rate have suggested[1] that it is primarily used

[1] See especially an article by Mr. Strawson in *Analysis* Vol. 9 No. 6, June 1949; and one by Mr. A. R. White entitled 'Truth as Appraisal', which appeared in *Mind* Vol. LXVI No. 263, July 1957.

in order to confirm or affirm. This suggestion is a less familiar one than that in the case of 'good', but it is nevertheless well worth looking into.

It is not difficult, of course, to think of some examples of the use of the word 'true' which this interpretation would fit very easily and well. Someone, for instance, who finds that his account of what has happened is doubted, may indignantly reply "It is perfectly true", reaffirming thereby what he had originally said. Or it may be someone else that comes to his aid with "What he said is quite true", in this way confirming the first speaker's version of the matter. In the same way a true theorem in logic or mathematics is quite simply a theorem that one is entitled to assert or to affirm. To say that the 'truth of the matter' is not known is to say that there is no account of it that can be affirmed with certainty; similarly a first tentative hypothesis may receive subsequent confirmation in some such phrase as "our suspicions have turned out to be true". And so on.

On the other hand, there is no denying that there are other examples of the use of the word 'true' which need a little forcing if they are to be interpreted in this way. If you cast doubts on something that I have said, I may indignantly reaffirm that it is 'perfectly true', but your dubious question "Is that really true?" is probably not intended as a simple request to know whether I am still prepared to confirm my original statement. And suppose I do reaffirm it and you persist in your doubts with "I still cannot believe that is true", how would you be using the word 'true' here? We could perhaps say that you are using it in order to indicate your own inability or refusal to affirm or confirm my story. But this would be awkward, because in the normal way of things no one is likely to say that the question of your positively affirming or confirming anything arose at all. There is a somewhat similar awkwardness involved if we try to interpret the promise made by a witness to tell the whole truth and nothing but the truth simply as a more

F

emphatic or, as one might say, a double way of affirming what he is about to say.

We might seem to be nearer the mark in all these cases if we interpreted 'true' as 'affirmable', meaning thereby something that one is justified in affirming. Thus your question "Is that really true?" might be interpreted as "Is one really justified in affirming that?"; and your reiterated doubt "I still cannot believe that is true" as "I still cannot believe one is justified in affirming that". But even this does not seem to be quite right. There are times when one might say "Although his affirmations were fully justified when he made them we are now in a very different position and can see that they were not true after all." At first sight this seems to suggest that one might sometimes be justified in affirming something that is not true; and if this is the case, our suggested interpretation of the word 'true' will no longer work at all, however much force we are prepared to use. For it would seem that if we stick to it, we shall find ourselves using such self-contradictory sentences as "Sometimes one is justified in affirming what one is not justified in affirming"; and this is clearly ridiculous. The situation is not quite as bad as that, however. For although we certainly can very reasonably say that what it was once justifiable to affirm is now no longer thought to be true, we can just as reasonably say that what was once thought to be true is now known not to be so. As far as standards of evidence are concerned[1], we are only justified in affirming something which we have every reason to *believe* to be true at the moment of affirmation; and though there is always, as a matter of logical necessity, the off-chance that we might be wrong, if we really do have every reason for believing it, we can neither need nor obtain any stronger justification. But now, having said that, we have emerged from one difficulty only to find ourselves faced with another. For how is the word 'true' to be interpreted in the last sentence but

[1] From other points of view, of course, it is quite common to find people justifying on occasion the telling of deliberate untruths.

one? If we replaced it with some such expression as 'affirmable' or 'justified by the evidence in affirming', we should get a sentence like "the evidence only justifies us in affirming something which we have every reason to believe that it justifies us in affirming at the moment of affirmation"; and this sentence manages to seem all at once more complicated, emptier and sillier than the one that it is intended to replace. If somebody asks us our reason for making a certain assertion and we reply "Because it happens to be true", we may at least suppose ourselves to be giving some genuine sort of reason and not merely to be dodging the question by making an emphatic reaffirmation in disguise.

This last point is a somewhat curious one. At first sight after all it might seem that to affirm something because it happens to be true is not merely to have 'some genuine sort of reason' for affirming it, but is actually to have one of the best reasons that one could possibly have. What better justification could I have for affirming, for example, that there are black swans in Australia than that there *are* black swans in Australia? The odd thing about this justification is, however, that, powerful as I may feel it to be, it will be of hardly any use at all to you if you are seriously doubtful about my assertion and want to know if and how it could be justified. If, really unconvinced, you ask me why I affirm that there are black swans in Australia and I merely reply "Because it happens to be true", you are not very likely to receive this as the best possible answer; you are much more likely to feel cheated and that it is no effective answer at all. Your obvious next question is "But how do you know that it is true?". There are clearly a great variety of things that I might reply to this; for example, "My Geography master says so", "I read it in the encyclopaedia", "My Australian aunt told me" or "I have seen them myself"[1]. But any of

[1] Of course you might further want to know why, for example, my Australian aunt is to be trusted; but we can assume for this context that you are prepared to take her as an authority. Otherwise we shall only complicate the matter without in fact raising any new issues.

these answers would have been just as likely to satisfy you as an answer to your first question as they will be to satisfy you as an answer to your second. That is to say, they seem to do equally well as answers to the question "How do you know it is true?" as to the question "What justifies you in affirming that?"; which suggests that the two questions may after all be very much the same.

It may help us to appreciate the peculiar status of "because it happens to be true" as a reason for affirming anything, if we turn for a moment to consider the association that exists between the terms 'true' and 'fact'. If you ask anybody at random what is the meaning of 'true', he is most likely to reply that to say that anything is true is to say it is 'in accord with the facts'; or something very similar. (This is also one of the answers given by the dictionary.) There is no doubt that in ordinary speech the partnership between the words 'true' and 'fact' is a very close one. Unfortunately, like so many of the associations to be found in the unsystematic language of everyday, this one may, if treated too systematically, lead to all sorts of paradoxical problems.

There would be no point in our trying to go into the various so called 'Theories of Truth' that have been produced and upheld by various philosophers[1], but there is just one of them that is worth mentioning here, that which is known as the Correspondence Theory, according to which an assertion is true if, and only if, it corresponds to a fact. This theory is worth mentioning because it arises precisely out of an attempt to build the everyday association between 'truth' and 'fact' into a systematic and consistent way of thought. This attempt has in fact given rise to many well-known puzzles; and many of them have arisen because of the number of different sorts of assertions that we should

[1] And not only philosophers. Theologians and artists are among others who have produced such theories. I should add that there are more fundamental difficulties in the way of the correspondence theory of truth than those that I mention here.

normally be prepared to call true or false, to which it is hard to say what sort of facts would correspond.

A few examples may help to make clear the difficulties in the way of systematising the relationship between true assertions and facts. How, for instance are we to deal with negative propositions? Are we to say that if and when they are true, they are so because they correspond to or are in accordance with some negative fact? Shall we say that if the propositions "John loves Mary" and "Mary is loved by John" are true, they correspond to two facts or one? And what, to take a somewhat more complicated example, shall we say of the three propositions "John loves Mary", "a man loves Mary" and "somebody loves Mary"? One fact or two or three? Another sort of difficulty arises in connection with what are often called truths of mathematics or of logic. There are many analytic propositions, especially perhaps those which occur in mathematics[1], which most people would be unhesitatingly prepared to call true. Are we to say that in view of the fundamental differences between synthetic and analytic propositions, the use of the term 'true', and with it that of 'fact', should be restricted to the former? Or, alternatively, that both sorts of propositions correspond when true to facts, but to facts of fundamentally different kinds? Or, again, that the association between 'facts' and 'true' must be broken, so that we may continue to speak of analytic propositions being true while denying that they correspond or even refer to any sort of fact? This is the solution which many empiricist philosophers of the present day explicitly or implicitly adopt[2]; for them the association between the notions of 'fact' and 'observation' overrides all other considerations. We must not expect,

---

[1] I assume here, as elsewhere in this book, that mathematical assertions are best treated as propositions. It is, of course, possible to argue, and some people do so argue, that the term 'proposition' should not be stretched in this way and that the nature of mathematical assertions should be described in some other manner, either by stretching different terms or by inventing completely new ones.

[2] See Chapter 2, page 11.

77

needless to say, to find any clear cut solution that will exactly reflect the far from clear cut vagaries of ordinary speech. Yet both this one and the more radical suggestion that the uses of 'true' and 'fact' should both be confined to synthetic propositions seem to place more of a strain on our accustomed ways of thinking and talking than does the suggestion that there may be as many kinds of fact as there are types of assertion that we are prepared to call true or false. On the other hand, to talk in this way of fundamentally different sorts of facts can be dangerously deceptive; it is a way of formulating the problem that can somehow easily get taken not as a formulation but as the answer.

We might, of course, start from the other direction and ask first what is the meaning of 'fact'. The usual sort of answer, and again it is to be found in the dictionary, is that a fact is whatever is the case, or more simply whatever is true. Normally, someone who says that a fact is something that is the case thinks of it as being the case irrespective of what anybody may think or feel about it. In very much the same way, ordinary people, and they presumably include the majority of even the most unordinary thinkers in their more ordinary moments, tend quite naturally to think of the world as a whole as being the way it is irrespective of how anyone thinks or feels. Once again this view would give rise to many difficulties if one tried to systematise it, and many partial qualifications would no doubt have to be made. But for most ordinary purposes the ordinary straight-forward view of the world as being what it is and of the facts as being what they are, whether one knows about them or not, whether one likes them or dislikes them, is the only sensible and justifiable view to take. We may add that one could say very much the same things of most expressions involving the notion of truth. For again it is commonly felt that the truth is as it is, whether one knows it or not and whether one likes it or not. To find out the truth of a matter is to find out the way it really is; it is to find out the facts.

All this may seem finally to establish the relationship

78

between 'true' and 'according to the facts' as expressions that are to all intents and purposes equivalent and inter-changeable. So why should one be liable to find oneself faced with embarrassing puzzles if one tries to systematise the equivalence? At least part of the explanation seems to be that in so far as 'the facts' refer to the way the world is, they not only confront us as things that are stubbornly and often inconveniently independent of us who are faced by them, but they appear, too, as things that are there, things that in some sense or other have a sort of positive existence and which together go to make up the world as it is[1]. No doubt we can quite happily make remarks like "The fact is that there was nothing there at all"; but we remain uneasy if actually challenged about negative facts, because they seem in some curious way to refer to nothing that is there to be a fact. Similarly, in spite of the obvious differences in meaning between the three sentences, we feel inclined to say that "John loves Mary", "a man loves Mary" and "somebody loves Mary" all refer to one and the same fact, because there is after all only the one thing actually going on in the world, namely the one case of somebody loving somebody else with which all three sentences may in their different ways be concerned.

The upshot of all this seems to be that when we say that something is true, we are strongly inclined to say too that it is a fact and, on that account, something that has some kind or other of positive and independent existence of its own. Yet at the same time we normally and naturally take to be true things that we should feel it very odd to reckon as positively and independently existing facts. It is, of course,

[1] One of the best known utterances of one of the best known philosophers of this century is "The world is the totality of facts". The philosopher in question (Ludwig Wittgenstein) later changed his mind, however, and came to think that his earlier remark had been ridiculous. This was very largely because he subsequently became exceedingly sensitive to the many difficulties, in the way of determining the exact relationships between language and the non-linguistic world.

I need hardly add that the word 'exist' would raise enough problems on its own if once we started to look into the matter.

very unusual for this underlying discrepancy actually to make itself felt—except perhaps in the case of value judgments; but this is a point to which we are coming in a moment. However it does seem to provide some solution to the problem, which we left hanging in the air, of the peculiar status as a reason for affirming anything of "because it happens to be true". For suppose that we translate the reason in question into "because it happens to be a fact". This, as we have just seen, can carry the suggestion that the fact concerned relates to something, or rather *is* something that really exists. As far as questions of truth and falsity are concerned, the only thing that can in the last resort fully and finally justify my assertion that there are black swans in Australia is that there should be black swans in Australia. In saying that this is a fact, I may seem to be providing this full and final justification. But, whatever I may hope or intend, the word 'fact' cannot really do the comical trick of providing the black swans themselves; all it actually provides, since no further information is disclosed, is a further affirmation of my original assertion.

Nevertheless, there are in ordinary speech too many differences between the family of words clustered around 'true' and the family of words clustered around 'affirm' for it to be possible simply to replace one set by the other without arousing feelings of discomfort. This is partly due to the effort that the word 'fact' seems to make to get beyond language and affirmations to the very things to which the affirmations refer, and to the way in which its associate 'true' may carry on occasions, though perhaps even more elusively, the same sort of suggestion. But quite apart from these particular associations, there remain sufficient differences to prevent an entirely smooth transition from one to the other. It would be reasonably straightforward if we could simply say that the truth as anyone sees it is that which he is prepared to affirm. But, even if we ignore the fact that people are prepared to make many affirmations which they do not in the least suppose to be

80

justified by the evidence, we still cannot say this exactly. For there is also the important difference between saying that something is true and saying that one is justified in affirming it on the available evidence, that is the difference between saying that to the best of one's *belief* something is the case and that one *knows* it to be the case. There is a similar difference between the phrases 'in the highest degree probable' and 'certain'; and while it is very important to point out that in one sense no synthetic proposition is certain in the same way as an analytic proposition, simply because it is always at least logically possible that the opposite of a synthetic proposition should be or should have been the case, the ordinary familiar use of the word 'certain' is not reserved for analytic propositions. It is true that one way of marking the distinction between analytic and synthetic propositions might be to place restrictions on the use of words like 'certain'. But we must remember that the language which would result from such restrictions would be different from the one in which we are all normally at home.

Thus to say that something is certain is normally to make a stronger claim than to say that it is as probable as it can possibly be; it is to offer a kind of guarantee that is not contained in the latter phrase and so to lay oneself open to much stronger reproach if one should turn out to be wrong. To say that something is true is likewise to affirm it in a special guaranteeing sort of way. But, of course, to guarantee an affirmation is not to provide a reason for it; anyone who genuinely doubts my affirmation that there are black swans in Australia and asks me why I say so, is asking not for a further guarantee, but for the grounds on which both guarantee and original affirmation may be based. Admittedly when we say that something is true, it feels as if we are doing more than merely affirming it even with a guarantee—though we are certainly doing that; it feels as though we are somehow describing it as 'rooted in reality'. But when we come to look at this latter phrase more closely, we see that although it embodies the common-sensible unreflecting assumption that there is a reality, a way things are and that is all there is to it, it presents us paradoxically with an illusion, the illusion that there is some material difference between finding out whether something is the case and finding out whether it is *really* the case. Furthermore, it is easy, as many people have found, to derive from this situation the suggestion that everything that we may say to be true must in one way or another belong as a fact to the one same reality; this is confusing because it suggests deep and wholly mysterious similarities between such different things as, for example, synthetic propositions, analytic propositions and value judgments, while obscuring the important fundamental differences that there are between them.

These differences are, of course, at the very centre of our concern in the whole of this book. Appropriately enough, seeing that we have found ourselves so concerned in this chapter with the ideas of confirmation and affirmation, it happens that an excellent way of expressing them is, in fact, to show the different ways in which the three classes of assertions may be attacked or confirmed. We have already glanced at this question with reference to synthetic and analytic propositions and seen how fundamentally different the ways of their confirmation are. Value judgments are different again; and to get some idea of the sort of thing that is involved, we may take one very sketchy example.

Suppose I find you picking primroses on the side of the road and tell you that you ought not to pick them there. You do not see why; after all, you saw me picking primroses a little further down the same road only yesterday. "Well", I explain, "if you go a little further down the road to pick them, nobody will notice that they have gone, but if you pick them here they will be missed". "So what?", you reply, "they do not belong to anybody". "It is quite true that they do not belong to anybody but", I explain again, "old Mrs. Brown can see these roadside primroses from her cottage window and, since she cannot get out nowadays, they are the only ones that she can see; and I know it gives her a great deal of pleasure". "So what?", you repeat, "I do not know Mrs. Brown". "But", I say, "surely it is just the same to you to go a few yards further on to pick your primroses. It makes a lot of difference to her; and one should always try to give pleasure to people". You are still obstinate and say that you do not see why she should not be perfectly satisfied with looking at the daffodils in her cottage garden. At this point I may try a different line of argument. "Do you agree", I may ask you, "that one should give the same treatment to other people as one would expect for oneself?" Yes, you accept that, but hastily and defensively add that you yourself would be just as satisfied looking at daffodils as at primroses. "That is as may be", I say, "but you would surely protest, wouldn't you, if somebody took away something which you like very much when he could quite easily have satisfied himself as well by taking something else". This is a proposition which you are almost bound to accept. "Well", I go on, "the fact of the matter is that, reasonably or unreasonably, Mrs. Brown does enjoy looking at primroses more than at daffodils and if you take them away when you can just as easily get primroses by walking a few paces further on, you are quite unnecessarily taking away something which gives her pleasure; and that is treating her in a way in which you have admitted that you would not yourself like to be treated by someone else".

There are various things to notice about this example. In the first place, I start off by trying to show you what is different about this case from other apparently similar cases of picking primroses. I have to do this, of course, in order to justify a different value judgment at all. Secondly, the reason I give for leaving the primroses where they are is simply that I approve of the end, giving pleasure to old Mrs. Brown, to which they are a means. Thirdly, I attempt to justify my view that it is a good thing to give pleasure to

Mrs. Brown by reference to the general principle that one should always try and give pleasure to people. Fourthly, when I see that working back to this general principle does not seem to make much impression on you, I make a fresh start in the reverse direction; I look first for a general principle that you do accept, and then try to show you that, although it may not originally have occurred to you, this case is one that comes under your own general principle. Fifthly, in order to show you how particular value judgments are related to more general principles and vice versa, I have at each stage to call your attention to the truth of certain purely factual statements, for example that Mrs. Brown prefers looking at primroses to looking at daffodils.

This is, of course, only one example and a very straightforward one at that. But at least it serves to illustrate the way in which value judgments are typically confirmable by showing what other value judgments are involved. This may involve referring back to more and more general principles or, if the value judgment is already fairly general, it may involve going in the other direction and showing what are the concrete cases to which the general principle would apply. There may, of course, be no explicit reference to general principles at all. I may justify a value judgment by showing that some other value judgment is involved, leaving the general principle that provides the formal link between the two cases to be tacitly understood. Nearly always reference to assertions that are not value-judgments, such as analytic or synthetic propositions, will be understood as well. Sometimes the point of this sort of justification is primarily to show that the particular value judgment is in accord with the speaker's own basic principles or outlook; sometimes the main point is to win agreement from one's listeners by appealing to their basic principles. In some cases it seems more natural to speak of affirmation or reaffirmation, at other times of confirmation and at yet other times, perhaps, it would not, as language is ordinarily used, be natural to speak of either even though the same sort of justificatory procedures are being used.

We may now at last come back to face directly the question as to the sense if any, in which value judgments may be said to be true. Our doubts arose because of the traditional connection between the terms 'true' and 'false' on the one hand and 'statement' or 'proposition' on the other, when we saw how difficult it would be to construe value judgments as statements. On the other hand we have seen that to say that something is true is always, in part at least, to confirm or affirm whatever is being asserted in a way that involves very special commitments or guarantees on the part of the speaker. Moreover, in saying that the differences between synthetic propositions, analytic propositions and value judgments can be expressed as differences between their ways of confirmation, we have laid our finger on at least one important thing that they do all have in common; though the relevant methods may be very different, they *are* all three open to confirmation and refutation. If, therefore, we were prepared to concentrate on the affirmatory or confirmatory aspects of the word "true", we should be able to give a completely coherent account of its use, according to which to say of anything that it is true is to commit oneself to maintaining it on whatever grounds may be most appropriate to the case and to offer a special sort of guarantee that the commitment is seriously undertaken. In particular to say that a value judgment is true would be to commit oneself to belief in and defence of that value judgment.

Of course this account of the word 'true' does deliberately ignore those other associations which, as we have seen, it so frequently has in ordinary speech. Nevertheless it has many advantages. It would be foolish to suppose that any account of such a central term as 'true' could be both coherent and at the same time faithful to all the nuances of ordinary language. We have seen that there are strong reasons for saying that the word 'true' is typically used to evaluate; and in this way we are able to give an account of its use as a value-word which will cover the wide range of its employment and which runs parallel to the account which we gave of the word 'good'. On this view, then, we may say that the meaning of 'true' lies in this special sort of affirmatory or confirmatory function that we have tried to describe, while the criteria on which such confirmations may be based will obviously vary, as in the case of 'good', from context to context. It follows that to say that it is true that such and such a thing is good, is to do exactly what one would be doing in saying that any other assertion was true; it is to affirm the assertion in question in a way that offers a fully committed guarantee.

It turns out, then, on the basis of this account that one may after all be perfectly justified in saying of value judgments that they may be true or false, even without having somehow to construe them as statements. Whether or not the interpretation of the word 'true' which allows us to do this will be satisfactory to all those who have wanted to insist that value judgments are statements and that values are properties, is another matter. In fact it is not very likely that it will satisfy them all. We have mentioned the widespread feeling that to say that something is a fact is to say that it is part of or "rooted in" a state of affairs that is "a reality", that "exists in its own right". Many people have somehow felt that their values would be secure and a firm purpose given to their lives only if these values too existed in their own right; if, that is to say, their validity were independent of anyone's thoughts or feelings, or language. At the same time, it would be possible, if there were as a *matter of fact* only one set of basic values, to say that people with radically different codes were as a *matter of fact* wrong; and to mean by that something that feels, naturally enough, a good deal more conclusive than does a "mere" reaffirmation of one's own values, however firm and however deliberately thought out. Hence the temptation to say that value judgments state facts and the desire to represent them as synthetic propositions. And, if we remember once again the nature of the association between 'true' and 'fact', we shall understand how this temptation and this desire may reinforce the feeling that if value judgments are not statements, to talk of their truth or falsity could be nothing but a mistake.

It should be added that the comfort that anyone may derive from falling into this temptation is only a comforting confusion. Commendations and confirmations must be made by somebody; value judgments must be somebody's value judgments. It may be consoling to transform personal principles into impersonal facts, but it is not really clear thinking[1]. In any case the fact that your principles are *your* principles or that the values of a community are the values of *that community* does not on its own go to show that either are therefore arbitrary. They may in the one case be based on profound study and involve a difficult and well thought out way of life or, in the other, represent the accumulated experience of many generations. Neither profound study nor accumulated experience provide, of course, infallible guarantees; but to describe the results of either of them as arbitrary would surely be very peculiar.

As a sort of postscript to this chapter, it may be as well to say just a word or two about the terms 'real' and 'reality', partly because we have had to use them a certain amount in the course of the discussion and partly because they are in many ways very similar to 'true'. In many contexts, of course, there is little to choose between the terms 'real' and

---

[1] I do not mean by this that all principles of evaluation are personal in the sense that they are personal to any given individual, but merely that they must be principles of persons.

Incidentally, I have noticed that many people seem to believe that there is some incompatibility between the sorts of arguments that I have been putting forward here and their religious beliefs. This is certainly not the place to become involved in any sort of discussion about religion. I should simply like to record that while particular religious formulations might well require reinterpretation, the idea that there is any basic incompatibility of this sort seems to me to be completely mistaken.

'genuine'. There are ways, however, in which 'genuine' is not quite so difficult to deal with as 'real' and so we may do best to look first at it and see what happens if we ask our by now familiar test question, whether it is possible to say of any two things that they may be exactly the same in every respect except only that where one of them is genuine the other is not. At first sight it seems as if this may indeed be possible. Two objects might be to all outward appearances exactly the same in shape, size and workmanship, but have been made one of them in an Indian village and the other in a Birmingham factory. It would be natural enough to say that the only difference between them lay in the genuineness of the first. But on second thoughts this can not be the only difference, for even to explain the situation we had to specify a difference in point of origin. 'Genuine' does not, of course, mean anything like 'originating in an Indian village'; it can be applied to a great variety of objects that have nothing whatsoever to do with India. One might, perhaps, try to account for it as a very much more generally descriptive term meaning something like 'being what it purports to be'. Thus the genuine Indian bowl is the one that was actually made in India; the genuine Rembrandt is the painting which was actually painted by Rembrandt. This is not an implausible account, but even so it will still only enable us to deal with a limited number of usages of the word 'genuine'. There are many imitations which do not, after all, purport to be anything else. The reputable jeweller who sells an imitation pearl necklace says quite explicitly that it is not made of genuine or real pearls. In this case and in many others like it the antithesis seems to be between what occurs naturally and is therefore counted as genuine and what is made by man and is therefore counted as artificial. (I have known a number of people who refuse to admit that tinned vegetables are genuine vegetables or to accept the genuineness of vitamins that come in pills.) On the other hand, there are cases where the antithesis is the other way round; "That is not a genuine ancient axe head" we may say, "but only a piece of flint that happens to have been shaped like an axe head by purely natural forces".

In this apparently confusing situation, it may seem at first sight that the word 'genuine' can mean first one thing and then another. But this is by now a familiar predicament and we should be prepared to follow the clue given by the fact that we are bound if we differentiate between two things on the grounds that one alone is genuine, to recognise at least some other difference between them, and seek to account for the ways in which the word is used on the basis of the distinction between meaning and criteria. It is not easy in fact, to find a formula for what might be called the meaning of 'genuine' on the basis of this distinction; there seems to be no convenient word like 'commendation' or more or less convenient word like 'affirmation', which we used in the two previous cases. The best term I can think of is one coined by somebody[1] who used the expression 'tick-word'. Thus we use the word 'genuine' to tick off, so to speak, whatever it is that we refer to as genuine, to tick it off as being an all round satisfactory representative of its class, whatever that class may be. It is hardly necessary to add that the criteria on the basis of which anything may be judged to be a satisfactory representative of its class are as various as the different ways in which things may be classified.

For very many contexts this account will, as we said, do as well for 'real' as for 'genuine'. It too is used as a 'tick-word', to underline whatever is being referred to as the supposedly most representative or most important member of its class. But it will be evident from the ways in which we have already used terms like 'reality' in this chapter that they, like 'facts', are associated with those very general ideas, so difficult to express clearly, of something that is actually there, existing in its own right. The term 'real' is especially associated with the age-old distinction between

[1] I cannot remember exactly who it was, and have not been able to find out.

appearance and reality, not just in particular contexts but generalised to apply to everything at once, according to which reality is thought of as that which in some sense or other underlies or is hidden behind appearance. This is one of those points in our language through which all sorts of ancient general metaphysical ideas about the nature of the world maintain an inarticulate hold upon our thought. Anything that we think that we see or touch or in any other way perceive may turn out to be deceptive, and in any case in the long run there is nothing in the world as we know it that is not subject to change. Yet, men cannot help feeling, underneath all this deception and change there must be something unchanging, in some way or other responsible for the world that we know. This, whatever it is, is the reality beneath appearances. It may itself never be open to direct observation, but it is responsible for the appearances that we are able to observe; it is what is permanent and lasting beneath everything that is temporary and transient. On both these counts it is natural to feel that it is the only thing that is in the long run of over-riding importance. So that we use for it the name of 'reality' is fully appropriate, for this sense of importance provides the link with the every-day employment of the term 'real' that we started by noting.

This is not the place to embark on a discussion of the merits and demerits of these sorts of 'metaphysical' beliefs. It is enough for us to note that they may sometimes give a sense to a word like 'real' that is not so much different from as additional to its more normal straight-forward evaluative function. In this the terms 'fact', 'real' and 'true' go together. It may not be possible to clarify completely this partly submerged aspect of their meaning, probably because there is nothing definite enough for complete clarification. But there is no getting away from the fact that in ordinary usage this aspect, though generally under the surface, is very often there.

The main points of this chapter may be summarised briefly enough. If we are prepared to agree that the word 'true' is used to evaluate and has as its meaning the function of indicating some sort of specially guaranteed affirmation or confirmation, we shall be able to give a coherent account of how value judgments may be said to be true or false without having to construe them as statements. Admittedly this view of the word 'true' fails to take into consideration certain aspects of its significance in ordinary speech. These aspects are concerned with the way in which it may sometimes be taken to refer, especially perhaps through its association with such other terms as 'fact' and 'real', to what we may call the nature of things as they are, existing in the way they do, independently of anyone's thoughts or feelings about them. These tend, however, to be very unclear allusions[1]; and in leaving them aside, our view of 'true' has the great advantage of being able to account both for the fundamental differences between synthetic propositions, analytic propositions and value judgments and for one of the most important points that they have in common. For all three types of assertion are open to attack or confirmation; but the different ways in which they may be confirmed or attacked are fundamental aspects of the ways in which they are all different from each other.

[1] By this I mean that they are very hard to work out in closely specified detail. But I do not, of course, want to say that nothing exists outside human thought—a view that to me is either unintelligible or false.

7

"CAN I BE SINCERELY MISTAKEN ABOUT WHAT IS RIGHT?"

I HOPE that the argument of the last five chapters will by now have become reasonably clear. But it is impossible to be completely sure about the force of an argument, however clear it may seem, until one has been able to work out its implications for matters with which it had not originally been concerned. This is true even if the argument is one's own. So it would be as well if we turn in this chapter to one such question which has not so far come up for direct consideration, but on which our previous discussion must obviously have some bearing.

The question I propose to take is whether it is possible to be sincerely mistaken in one's views as to what is right[1]. One of the interesting things about this question is that I have known people to agree at once that the answer to it was obvious, and then discover to their surprise that the answers they gave were different. It is clear enough that one can be sincerely mistaken in one's view of the facts; and hence people who think of values as some sort of fact can readily understand that one should be sincerely mistaken about values. On the other hand, people who have thought of value judgments as being essentially matters of feeling or taste cannot see what there is to be mistaken about; you may like spinach, I may not, but there is no sense in saying that either of us is right or wrong. This is quite a common view, and one that has seemed particularly scandalous to

[1] Mistaken not about the relevant facts—i.e. in terms of the example of the last chapter, Mrs. Brown doesn't really like primroses at all,—but as to the matters of principle involved.

objectivists[1], who have felt that if values did not somehow have an independent status of their own, then anything that anybody did must be right provided only that he believed it to be so. Someone who accepts the sort of arguments that I have been putting forward may indeed hold this kind of view. But he is not, I think, bound to; not at any rate in this simple, extreme form.

Before tackling the question directly, there is one preliminary point to be noted. All the discussion so far has centred round the word 'good'. For our present purposes we may be justified in saying no more about the word 'right' than that it is a value word with a function very similar to that of 'good'. But in saying this we should not forget that the two words are seldom interchangeable without any shift of meaning and that in some contexts we may deliberately want to contrast them. In some ways, indeed, the relations between them can be extremely varied and tricky, and it would be absurd to pretend that they can be given by any simple formula. People have written whole books to put forward their views on this subject, and to express their disagreement with other people's books. Sometimes the differences between the two terms may involve important points of substance; in other contexts they may turn out to be largely a matter of local English idiom. Here, at any rate, it is just worth noticing as a very general indication that the word 'right' has particularly close association with the notions of 'law' or 'rule', and that its application therefore is usually somewhat more restricted than that of its partner 'good'. Something that is right is something that is in accordance with the relevant rule; we may talk of "the right way to dress for Ascot" (or, for that matter, "the right way to go down a coal mine"), "the right way to fill in a form", "the right way to behave". At the same time the notion of what is right is closely

---

[1] That is to say people who "claim that the truth or falsity of moral judgment depends wholly on the nature of the *objects* which they are about and not on the subject who makes them". See Chapter 3, p. 21.

connected with the notion of what fits the case; "Smith is the best of many good men, none of whom however are exactly right for the job". The word 'good' is used to commend; 'right' is usually used to commend with respect to a much more specific situation. Or perhaps a better way of putting this would be to to say that 'right' is used to commend in much more specific respect to the whole contextual situation. To say that something is right is generally to say that it is the sort of thing that the situation demands. "Although he may have had the best of intentions, what he did was not the right thing to do"; that is to say that his action cannot be commended with respect to the particular situation, even though one may in a way commend him for doing it in so far as it is taken as a general manifestation of character.

(There are, of course, contexts in which to say that something or some form of behaviour is right seems much less like evaluating it than describing it as being of the sort that is enjoined by some particular set of rules. Indeed in a context where the rules are quite definite and specific and where any question as to the value of obeying them is left entirely open, to say of an action that it is or is not in accordance with the rules *is* simply to describe it. As a matter of fact, it is comparatively unusual in such contexts to use the word 'right' alone; we are more likely to say, for instance, "what he did was legally right", using the word 'legally' to indicate the rules we were referring to. There is a very close analogy between this sort of situation and the sort of situation to which I have already referred in Chapter 5, p. 61.)

However, to come back to the main question. The first thing to notice is perhaps that when somebody says that the right thing to do is always what one believes oneself to be right, he may mean one of at least two very different things. He may, on the one hand, be the sort of extreme relativist who sees no sense in value judgments as such[1] and whose assertion that everybody's view of what is right is as good as everybody else's is in effect a despairing paradoxical way of

[1] As opposed, for example, to expressions of liking or distaste.

saying that there is no point in talking about them as right at all. On the other hand, he may in fact believe that the one thing that matters is sincerity and that people should always try to act on their own principles, however much he may himself disapprove of the principles in question. Thus people sometimes say that though they intensely dislike everything that Hitler did, he was nevertheless, on the assumption that he was sincerely trying to do what *he* thought he ought to do, quite right to act in that way. It is after all a possible and intelligible view to value sincerity above anything else. Moreover, there is no reason why someone who holds this view should not actively oppose other people with different principles from his own, as long as he does not blame them for acting as they do. He might perhaps have said to someone like Hitler "If you believe you ought to liquidate the Jews, you would be wrong not to try to do so, and I, for my part, would be equally wrong not to try to liquidate you for trying". (If this example seems excessively peculiar, consider the relative positions of spy and counter-espionage agent if both are sincere and patriotic men.) All that this comes to is that one can disapprove of somebody else's principles, while yet thinking, that since they are *his principles, he* ought to act up to them. And there is not really anything particularly strange or difficult about this.

This, however, has not got us much further on. For whether or not one believes that in the last resort the right thing for anybody else to do is whatever he thinks is right, however eccentric or unpleasant for all those who may be concerned, the question still remains whether he can be sincerely mistaken. People do, of course, say of others such things as "although he may think he is acting for the best, what he is doing is in fact completely wrong", and there is no denying that very often when they say things like this, they are assuming in some more or less vague or incoherent way that what is right and what is wrong are facts of which one may be aware or ignorant. But I can quite intelligibly disapprove of somebody else's principles or actions even though I may not suppose that my standards of value are facts in any other sense than facts about me and my standards (and, of course, anyone else who may happen to share them). What is more, I may be able to put forward reasons for my disapproval in the sort of way I sketched in the last chapter. No doubt, the other person may no more accept my justificatory reasons than he accepted my initial disapproval; and it is true that if I can find no common ground with him at any point at all, then there is no way in which I can finally prove to him that my viewpoint is better than his. I can even use phrases like "he may think that he ought to act in this way, but in fact he is wrong and he ought not to" as long as I remember that there are all sorts of suggestions contained in the phrase 'in fact' and that some of them may lead to the most complicated muddles if followed up in this context. In saying that "in fact he is wrong", I should not be understood as reverting to a view of values, or standards of values, as fact, but simply as affirming my own standpoint in a particularly definite sort of way. And indeed if I take my own standpoint seriously, there is every reason why I should do this. The fact that if you and I have completely different outlooks on life, there will be no way for either of us to prove that the other's is wrong, does not mean that we should consider these differences as of no more importance than mere differences in taste[1].

[1] It may be worth while to refer back to what I said in Chapter 5, pp. 64 ff. about the differences between value judgments on the one hand and expressions or assertions of like or dislike on the other. One of the differences between the two that I did not point out is that, as a general rule, one's likes and dislikes are logically independent of each other in a way that one's value judgments are not. Value judgments belong to some more or less rational structure, they depend on principles or standards and in this way commit anyone who takes them seriously to at least an attempt at consistency. I may dislike onion soup today and change my mind tomorrow and leave the whole of my other likes and dislikes unchanged; but if today I disapprove of something as a matter of principle, whatever the principle may be, then if I change my mind about it, I am bound to change my mind about everything else to which the same reasons might apply.

But see also Chapter 10, pp. 141 ff.

But if somebody else can (be said to) be wrong in his views as to what he ought to do, what about myself? At first sight it might seem to be excessively arrogant to suggest that I am the only person who is not liable to error in this way. It would be more modest to admit "Although I think I ought to do X, I may of course be wrong." But what exactly does this last sentence mean? If when I make a value judgment, I am thereby appealing to some standard or principle, to what other standard or principle can I in the same breath appeal from myself? Of course, people do say often "I think I ought to do X, but I am not completely sure", or make a definite distinction between the sentence "I ought to do X" on the one hand and "I think I ought to do X" on the other. But the apparent analogy from "he thinks he ought to do X" to "I think I ought to do X" can be very misleading. For the phrase 'I think' is probably less often used as a simple way of reporting what one thinks oneself as opposed to somebody else, than it is as a way of indicating that one's assertion is only tentative. "I think I ought to do X, but I am not quite sure; on further reflection I may change my mind." And if I do change my mind, I may then say "I thought I ought to do X, but I was mistaken"—'mistaken', of course not in the sense of being mistaken about a fact, but in the sense that I now disapprove of my previous point of view, and presumably, since this is a matter of value judgment, have reasons for my new position. In fact, assertions about one's own past self do in many ways resemble assertions about other people; (sometimes one's own past self may seem, on looking back, far more strange and incomprehensible than some other person whom one now knows extremely well).

So the up-shot of this is that it is possible both to disapprove of somebody else's standards and to say so, and to disapprove of the standards one once held oneself. But what one cannot do is to disapprove at a given moment of the standards one holds at that moment; for to disapprove of them would be to disapprove of them by reference to another set of standards and *these* would now be the standards one held. (It is not surprising that the last sentence is something of a tongue-twister as it is trying to express the self-contradictriness of a self-contradictory position.) I should add, of course, that in talking about one's own personal standards in this way, I am not necessarily suggesting that they are anything exceptional or private to the individual. It may be that I fully accept the standards of my Church, Party or any other group, and if so, these will be my own personal standards.

This last point is one that is worth insisting on, particularly as it may have seemed that there is in many cases where an authority is accepted an obvious answer to my rhetorical question, in the last paragraph but one, asking "to what standard or principle can I appeal from myself?". For it does not follow that because a person fully accepts the standards of some body external to or, at any rate, greater than himself, he will therefore be at all times fully aware of precisely what these standards are. This is in fact a very common situation; it is likely to arise whenever allegiance to a group or institution is expressed in the acceptance of some very general principle—whose precise implication nobody at all may yet have worked out with respect to every situation[1]. It is only too easy to accept a formula (including incidentally one of one's own invention) and to say, even to believe, that one believes it and yet hardly be able to say what it is that one believes beyond repeating the formula. Thus, there must be many people who know what it is to say, in the sort of unexpected and new situation in which they may be forced at least provisionally to make up their minds for themselves, "I think this is what I ought to do, but I cannot be sure until I have asked . . "; and the dots may be filled in by the name of a parent, or Party leader, priest, psychiatrist, or—and, did one but know it, one could

[1] In fact it would be more accurate to say that nobody at all *could* work out in advance the precise implications of very general principles for every conceivable situation that might occur.

probably extend the list by a quite remarkable variety of names.

In point of fact there are probably far more people who are, in the last resort, prepared to accept the authority of somebody else's judgment[1] than there are prepared to take full responsibility for themselves. Some of them may no doubt believe that the standards of whatever authority it is that they accept for themselves have some factual independence of that authority, in the sense that they regard the authority as a discoverer and a declarer of the standards, but not as their author. People who do believe this believe, in in my view, in a muddle, for reasons that I have already tried to explain. But one may perfectly well be fully committed to the acceptance of some authority, while realizing that whatever standards it may hold and advocate can be thought of only as a fact about that authority and cannot themselves have their own independent existence. A man may be prepared to accept his authority's standards as his own on a quite general basis; not because he thinks he ought to accept (for this would be to appeal to another standard), but simply because he does. It might be as if he were prepared to give to the authority a blank cheque for the making of any particular value judgments on which the authority might decide, committing himself thereby to honour his cheque however it was subsequently filled in.

A man of this sort, finding himself in a sort of situation with which he has not previously had to deal and where there is to his knowledge no existing pronouncement as to the proper course to take, will in effect be forced to guess as best he may as to how his cheque will be filled in when it comes back from headquarters. He may perhaps feel entirely confident as to what the result will be. But however confident he is and however good the reasons may be that he has for his confidence, it must remain possible, at any rate logically possible, that when the cheque does come

[1] By 'somebody else' I do not, of course, necessarily mean just one other individual person.

back he should turn out to have been wrong. This is so simply because the way in which the cheque is filled in is a fact, a fact about the decision that is actually taken by the authorities, and like any other fact expressible in a synthetic proposition; and, as you will remember, the only final way of determining the truth or falsity of a synthetic proposition is on the basis of observing the facts which it is about. Thus when such a man says, if he does, "I am convinced that I ought to do X, although it is, of course, just possible that I may be wrong", the possibility he is referring to is the possibility of having made a mistaken estimate of the facts about his authority. It is as if he had in this particular situation two standards; a provisional standard improvised by himself alone on the basis of his past experience and the overriding standard of the Party or Church, which is also his own standard in so far as he is fully committed to the body in question.

Perhaps the matter can be put like this. A man who is committed to acceptance of some authority in, for instance, matters of morals, may, even must, whenever he is uncertain consider seriously the possibility of his own provisional evaluations turning out to be wrong. By 'uncertain' I here mean 'uncertain as to the precise verdict of authority' and by 'wrong' 'wrong according to that verdict'; and he could say "wrong as a matter of fact" in so far as 'fact' refers to the views that authority holds. But if his provisional evaluation turns out to be as a matter of fact wrong in this way, it does so only by virtue of *his* acceptance of authority. It is a fact that his authority says so; but that their verdict is relevant to him depends on his own acceptance of it. Thus if we asked him about his basic principles, he would have in the last instance to reply not, as others might do, by reference to some such formula as 'the general happiness', but that his basic principle was to accept and endorse whatever judgments his authority made.

Somebody who is in the sort of position that we have just been discussing might prefer to express it by saying "I am

100

no maker of individual standards, for my part I am content to accept the standards which I have been taught and which I know are right". There is a point in expressing the matter in this way; to do so emphasises the important fact that the individual considered as an autonomous maker of standards is, if not wholly fictitious, at any rate very much an exception. But this does not mean that the individual has no share of responsibility for his standards whatsoever. For what can he mean by saying that the standards he accepts are right; 'right' is still a value word and what are the standards to which it in its turn refers? Perhaps there is no straightforward answer to this question. One cannot say that it refers to the standards of the authority for it is they that are under judgment. But neither would it be altogether fair to say that it refers to the standards of the individual setting himself up, even though at this one point alone, as a judge of the authority he accepts; for to say this would be, in many cases at any rate, to underrate the quality of the acceptance. So we are left to repeat that the only way of understanding his assertion is as a reaffirmation of the authority's standards as his own, that is to say as an outward expression of his identification of the two.

The whole question of the individual's acceptance of authority is admittedly an extremely difficult one to deal with satisfactorily within the sort of philosophical framework about which and out of which I am writing. This position is in many ways bound up with a pervading emphasis on the importance of the individual as such; and certainly moral philosophers have not recently paid as much attention to the problem of authority as very probably they should have done. In particular they seem to have underrated the importance of the way in which the most common standards are generally first taught and learnt as if they *were* simply facts. This is a point which will crop up again in the chapters that follow. But meanwhile it is as well to remember that even a man who accepts no authority other than his own may well be uncertain in a complex situation of the bearing upon it of his own general principles. This is a very understandable uncertainty, because the steps between a general principle and one specific value judgment are often exceedingly complicated. If we are serious in distinguishing value judgments from pure likes or dislikes on the basis that value judgments are always connected with reasons, then we should not find it surprising that such judgments cannot always be worked out at a moment's notice. Indeed a man who recognises no external authority may quite often take longer and be more hesitant in making up his mind in a particular situation than the one who relies on a well-recognised and comparatively well worked-out system of principles and their applications.

After all this, it is very probable that someone will still want to protest that though it must perhaps be conceded that one cannot at a given moment disapprove of the very standards that one holds at that moment, nevertheless one's standards might be wrong; for, he may insist, the mere fact of my own complete and sincere conviction is not enough to guarantee that my conviction is right. To try and answer this protest would in effect be to re-enter the argument at the same point in the circle at which we have already once begun; we should have to ask for the further standard to which the protest makes indirect appeal, which should be becoming by this time a fairly familiar question. All the same it is very natural that someone should want to protest in this way. For one thing, although I have kept on referring to 'my standards' and the impossibility of judging them all at once (as if I could both get outside and remain within them at one and the same time), nevertheless in a discussion like the present one, one never really seems to be discussing one's own standards as one holds them at the time of speaking. One talks about them certainly, but, it seems, only by way of example. The phrase 'my standards' refers to the standards of anyone who might be speaking in the first person. In this way the whole discussion seems to become completely impersonal, and, as we have already noted, there is no difficulty at all in the idea that one might disapprove of any and all other standards than those one holds oneself. For another thing, we have to remember that the distinction between values and facts is one that is blurred by many of the presuppositions of everyday speech and thought, and it is not easy for anyone, not even the most sophisticated philosopher, to remember to adjust all his ideas about value judgments to one consistent style. And finally, anyway, the admission of the possibility that one's own (present) standards may be wrong can be understood as the mark of an open mind; not necessarily by any means a vacillating or indecisive mind, but one belonging to someone who is always willing to consider seriously any fresh arguments that may be put to him and prepared, if it seems appropriate, to think through his standards again in any new situation that may crop up. From this point of view to say "perhaps my present standards may be wrong" can be understood as a reference to the quite intelligible possibility that I may at some future time revise my position; and from a revised position and a revised set of standards I may of course then condemn the standards that I once held, that is to say standards that I do as a matter of fact hold at the present moment.

I must now try and sum up what has been said in this chapter. We started with the assumption that 'right' is a value word, similar in many ways to the word 'good', but generally with a more specific function. However, we did not embark on any lengthy discussion of the various distinctions which these two terms may in certain contexts be used to mark, but instead took up the question whether it is possible for anyone to be sincerely mistaken in his views as to the proper values to hold and pursue. Clearly it would be quite inconsistent with the whole previous argument to allow that somebody's value judgment could be wrong as a matter of fact in that sense of the word which is linked with synthetic propositions. But in so far as phrases like 'in fact' are used in the ways in which I have suggested that the word 'true' is frequently used, namely to affirm or reaffirm in a peculiarly emphatic sort of way, then to say that somebody else's standards are wrong becomes a perfectly intelligible way of disassociating oneself from them. And the same is true of one's own past standards of value. The position is considerably more tricky and harder to make clear when one is dealing with someone who is completely committed to the acceptance of some other authority than himself alone. But even here the fact of such a commitment is to render the standards of the authority at the same time his own personal standards. And it remains true that while anyone may naturally be uncertain as to the precise implications of his most fundamental principles in a particular complex situation, nevertheless it is not possible for him to get outside and judge *all* his standards at once.

8

'OUGHT' AND 'IS' (i)—A MATTER OF LOGIC ?

FOUR chapters ago I raised, but did not answer, the question whether the slogan "An 'ought' can never be derived from an 'is' " is analytic or synthetic. It is time now to turn back to this question. As I said in that chapter, the distinction between evaluation and description is fundamental to the whole of our argument; and this, whether I had said it or not, must by now be patently evident. Description on the one hand and evaluation on the other, fact and value, statement and value judgment; all of these distinctions, on which I have been placing so much weight, are summed up in the alleged impossibility of deriving[1] an 'ought' from an 'is'. So if this *is* supposed to be impossible, we need to be quite clear why.

I have, of course, already tried to give a number of reasons why values should not be regarded as properties, why value judgments should not be construed as propositions, and why we should not expect value judgments and statements of fact to be open to justification, confirmation or attack in precisely the same way as each other. But in doing so, I had on page 55 for example to concede that "I would not claim that the arguments I have so far put forward actually prove that value judgments are not embodied in synthetic propositions. The effect of my arguments is cumulative but

[1] The word 'derive' in this context refers, of course, to analytic or logical derivations; derivations in the strict sense according to which no one who had properly understood the meanings of all the terms in the argument could consistently deny its validity without finding himself talking nonsense. In such an argument the conclusion follows *necessarily* from the premises—in that sense of the word 'necessary' which was introduced at the same time as the word 'analytic'.

even so, if one is sufficiently ingenious one may still produce enough counter-suggestions to fight further delaying actions." It is true that the further gist of the paragraph was to affirm once again that the recognition of a distinction between what I have been calling evaluation and description is fundamental; for, as I said, "if it is insisted that goodness is a property and that to call anything good is essentially to offer descriptive information about it, we shall need some other means of commending things once described. We cannot have it both ways at once". But the question remains—why should we recognise this distinction? Why shouldn't a description be a commendation at the same time?

One very common answer is that we must recognise the distinction as a matter of logic. Indeed, this is an answer that is so very often given and insisted upon that we ought to examine it for that reason alone, even if it did not raise the many important points that it does. So this chapter will be spent in considering the thesis that to derive an 'ought' from an 'is' is to commit a logical mistake.

There is one question, however, which should be dealt with before anything else. It may well occur to someone to ask whether it comes to the same thing to say, on the one hand, that "an 'ought' can never be derived from an 'is' " is an analytic proposition and, on the other, that its truth is a matter of logic. Some sort of answer to this question may in fact already be found in Chapter 3 where the term 'analytic' was first introduced. But it is only right to add that the key terms 'analytic' and 'logic' have been used in so many slightly different ways that there is not really any one straightforward cut and dried answer to be given. Some people certainly have used the term 'logic' in such a way that any matter concerned solely with the rules governing the mutual relations of different linguistic expressions is a matter of logic, and any argument based on these relations a purely logical argument—whatever the expressions in question may be. Many others, however, have preferred to restrict the use of the term to the study of what are called purely formal relationships, that is to say relationships depending on the meanings of such terms as 'and', 'or', 'not', 'if . . . then', 'all', and 'some'. On their view, logic is only concerned with the form or structure of arguments, with the ways in which arguments are built up, wholly irrespective of what they may be about and without restriction to any particular context. Take, for example, the sentences: (i) "All parents have or have had children" and (ii) "if X is either red or blue and it is not red, then it is blue". The great majority of philosophers would agree that both of these assertions are analytic, except perhaps for the purposes of some exceptional and extraordinary context. But on the stricter view I have mentioned, only the second is true on logical grounds. This is because the truth of the first assertion (about parents) has no application beyond the one particular context. In the second, on the other hand, 'X' can stand for anything whatsoever (while one can also, for that matter, substitute any other two adjectives for the words 'red' and 'blue'). The truth of this assertion depends simply on the meanings and mutual relations of the so-called logical connectives, 'or', 'and', 'if . . . then', so-called because they are basic connecting links in any chain of argument, whose very meanings lie in the different ways they connect phrases to each other.

It goes without saying that this is a very over-simplified view of a highly complex matter. But the important thing here is simply to be aware of the existence of such divergent views. For our own purposes it is more convenient to take the broader one and to regard all arguments that depend exclusively for their validity on the meanings and mutual relationships of different parts of language as logical arguments. This is anyhow probably fairly close to ordinary usage. If people do too great a violence to the rules governing the meaning of the words they use, if they talk too 'illogically', they risk not being understood. If, for example, I said of a

107

couple who were known neither to have children nor to wish to have them, that they were excellent parents, I could surely only be understood as having made a mistake in referring to them and not some other couple—or alternatively not understood at all; in ignoring the 'logic' of the word 'parents', I should fail to be talking sense[1]. So as far as we are concerned we may say that if it can be shown that to derive an 'ought' from an 'is' would be to break some rule of logic in the wider sense of that word, then this will have answered the question in which we are interested.

As soon as a reference is made to logic we have to be more than ever careful about how we talk; and the next point to note is that as soon as we look more closely, it becomes fairly obvious that the slogan about 'ought' and 'is' cannot itself be more than a slogan, and cannot be interpreted literally. For there are after all many value judgments in which the word 'is' appears rather than the word 'ought', and, conversely, many statements of fact which make use of 'ought' rather than of 'is'. "This is good" or "this is his duty" will do as examples of the one; "according to the weather forecast it ought to have been raining by now" as an example of the other. Nobody would quarrel about deriving the sentence "he ought to do X", from the sentence "X is his duty", for this is simply an example of one formulation of a value judgment being derived from another. On the other hand, one could well object to the inference that because according to Smith, Brown ought to do Y, it

---

[1] There may as usual be certain very special contexts in which my remark might be neither mistaken nor senseless; for instance, a context in which the word 'parent' referred to some institutional arrangement in some sort of school for children, grown-ups, or even perhaps animals. (Even here, of course, there would be the suggestion that the animals are from some point of view *as if* in the position of children.) But I have already explained three or four chapters ago that in the last resort it is impossible to fix any final meaning on to any collection of words considered wholly in abstraction from the particular context in which they are used.

follows that he ought really[1] to do it. So the point at issue is rather whether it is true, as Professor Popper has said, that "perhaps the simplest and most important point about ethics is purely logical, I mean the impossibility to derive non-tautological rules—imperatives, principles of policy, aims or however we may describe them—from statements of fact"[2].

If we are not to treat the slogan literally, then the particular form of the question to which I returned at the beginning of this chapter will clearly need to be modified. *If* taken literally, the slogan would, as we have just seen, be straight-forwardly false, since there is no doubt that sentences containing 'ought' can quite often be properly derived from one or more sentences containing no other verb but 'is'. But this strictly verbal interpretation is not very much to the point. It would be better to adapt our question along the lines of the quotation from Professor Popper and ask instead whether the assertion that it is impossible to derive value judgments from statements of fact is to be treated as analytic or synthetic. This is not only clearer; it is also the interpretation of the slogan that we actually took for granted when it was mentioned on page 43[3]. But even in this form it is an awkward question to handle, and we may well be puzzled to know where exactly to start. For how *does* one decide in such a case whether an assertion is analytic or synthetic, whether this 'most important point about ethics' is purely logical? And since this question is very much disputed we should probably do best not to plunge straight in before looking at one or two assertions which are fairly similar, but which can be shown to be based on logic in a reasonably obvious sense.

---

[1] With all the previous warnings and qualifications about the use in such contexts of a word like 'really' being borne carefully in mind.

[2] In his paper on "What can Logic do for Philosophy?" in the Aristotelian Society Supplementary Volume No. XXII 1948, p. 154.

[3] But even this formulation can only be used subject to certain reservations. (See the second section of Chapter 11.)

We may take for one example the well-known doctrine which, to express it in a brief and technical form, states that no universal statement can be deduced from a particular. Universal statements are statements about *all* of something or other; particular statements are statements about just *some* of whatever it may be. What the doctrine means is simply that there can be no formally watertight justification for making assertions about a whole class of objects or people merely on the basis of what is known about some of them. Suppose, once again, that one is talking about swans and says that all swans are white, making it clear that this assertion is intended to be a synthetic proposition and that no black-looking bird would be disqualified simply on the basis of the meaning of the word 'swan'. One may perhaps have seen a very great number of swans and all of them may have been white. But to be *logically* justified in asserting that all swans are white as the conclusion of a deductive argument, one's premises would have to refer to all the swans there are or ever will be. For if one's experience is limited to some members of a group, then it is always possible that among the remaining members there should be some of whom one's experience up to date might turn out to be misleading, even though that experience may have been of a very large majority indeed. Practical justification is, of course, another matter; when the matter is urgent, we may often be justified on practical grounds in acting on incomplete evidence, or even on no evidence at all. Indeed, evidence which is in this rather peculiar sense logically incomplete, may often still be very good. There are many universal generalisations which it would in practice seem ridiculous to dispute. All the same, if the evidence on which they are based is at all limited in this way, then it will always make sense to wonder whether a future observation will provide an exception to the rule. And it is fair to call this doctrine a logical one, because it is based on the very meanings of the words 'all' and 'some'. Nobody who had reflected about the matter could dispute its validity, if he were using these two keys words in the normally accepted way[1].

Another well-known logical thesis, which will do very well as an example (and which has at the same time some relevance to our purposes in this chapter), is the thesis that nothing can appear in the conclusion of a valid deductive argument which is not contained in the premises. This too may sound an obscure and technical thing to say, but the idea behind it should already be more or less familiar. You may remember that when I was trying to introduce the terms 'analytic' and 'synthetic', I said (half way down page 24) "there is a sense, it was held, in which an analytic proposition would bring no new information. To anyone who had properly understood the subject . . . the explicit setting out of the results of analysis in the full subject predicate form would be superfluous". Now, a deductive argument is one that is based exclusively on the meanings of certain key terms; (most typically perhaps, as I mentioned above, terms such as 'and' and 'if . . . then', but, of course, any term whatsoever could turn out to be the key term in a particular instance). If we look at it in this way, we can think of a valid deductive argument as being a sort of very long analytic proposition, its truth depending on the meanings of the central terms within it. From this point of view it should not be too difficult to see why nothing can appear in a conclusion of a valid deductive argument which is not 'contained' in the premises. It is because there is a sense in which anyone who fully understood the meanings of the premises, would thereby understand all the implications of the terms contained within them; fully to understand the meaning of a term is to understand the relation-

[1] For a conclusion to be validly deducible from any given premises, it must be logically impossible for the premises to be true and the conclusion to be false within the rules governing the meanings of all the relevant key terms. But there is nothing incompatible between the sentences "some swans are white" and "not all swans are white", however many may be the swans to which the first sentence refers. For what is meant by the phrase 'logically impossible', see Chapter 3, pp. 25-27.

ships into which it can enter with any other terms. So anyone who has understood the premise, has in this rather special sense understood the conclusion in advance of its being explicitly set out. As we said in that earlier chapter, a complicated analytic proposition may very well appear surprising; but to the theoretically perfect intelligence who has already understood the subject, it brings no new information. So the fact that nothing can appear in the conclusion of a valid deductive argument that was not contained in the premises may be said to hinge on the meanings given to such terms as 'deductive' and 'analytic'.

If we now take the last two examples together, we can say that the reason why it is not permissible to deduce a universal statement from a particular is because premises which refer only to some members of a group or class do not contain the necessary information about them all taken together. And in a similar way, if it is agreed that there *is* a distinction between evaluation and description, such that each is different from and essentially independent of the other, then premises which contain only descriptions will not ipso facto contain any evaluation that can validly turn up in the conclusion. To this extent it is true that it is a matter of logic that no value judgment can be derived simply from statements of fact—*if*, of course, the distinction really exists. But then it is still the fact that there is such a distinction that we need finally to establish.

This seems to leave the matter very much where it was. However, one thing at any rate has by now become fairly clear; there can be no way of basing the distinction we are after on the completely general notion of a valid deductive argument. Nor can it be based on the commonly accepted meanings of some pair of words like 'all' and 'some'; we have already seen that it is impossible to interpret the slogan about 'ought' and 'is' in this straightforward sense. There are too many different ways of expressing value judgments and statements of fact for anything as simple or convenient as that. So if there is any way of showing that the distinction is so closely woven into the common meaning of words that it can only be ignored at the cost of contradicting oneself into talking nonsense, to formulate it is likely to involve us in quite considerable complications.

At this stage somebody might very well ask why we should not be content to recognise the existence of the distinction and stop making such a fuss about trying to prove it as a matter of logic. Indeed, this is in my view what in the end we must do. All the same the desire to see it established on a so-called logical basis should not be thought of as frivolous or influenced by nothing but considerations of professional pedantry. It may sometimes be unavoidable, but it is never entirely satisfactory to rest an important argument on people's own personal impressions of their attitudes, thoughts or activities. What one person finds inconceivable, another may envisage as a perfectly intelligible possibility; where one may see a distinction, another may see a fundamental identity. This has been well put by one philosopher who, trying to maintain the existence of the distinction between value judgments and statements of fact on purely logical grounds, referred to his "desire to support the pronouncements I wish to make about value judgments by referring to considerations which are plain for all to see". For, as he went on to say, "I do not like having to say to people 'you know what it is to do this on the one hand, and that on the other', to fall back on asking them to reflect and see if I am not right. I would much rather draw their consideration to the facts about the way they speak"[1]. And this is, I think, a very understandable and, where applicable, progressive point of view. It is always better to appeal, when one can, to evidence that is in principle equally accessible to any informed and unprejudiced observer.

---

[1] The philosopher in question is Mr. R. F. Atkinson, and the quotation comes from a paper entitled " 'Ought' and 'Is' " in which we together put forward our respective arguments on the points I am discussing in this chapter. (The paper appeared in *Philosophy*, Vol. XXXIII, No. 124, Jan. 1958.)

The extent to which I sympathise with this outlook is, indeed, shown by the fact that the whole method of argument in this book has been based on discussions of the different ways in which words are or might be used. But though it has been possible to point out a number of differences between the ways in which we use typical value-words like 'good' or 'ought' on the one hand, and such typical descriptive or factual words as 'red' or 'kill' on the other, I have, as I have admitted, never been able to claim that these differences are by themselves conclusive. One trouble is that there can be an awkwardly large number of exceptions. Too often one is forced to say that either a descriptive or an evaluative word is not being used in its typical primarily descriptive or evaluative way; and if one is appealing to the facts of common usage alone, with no sort of reference to an independently understood distinction, one's appeal starts to lose its plausibility if the exceptions are too many. Moreover, the appeal to the ways in which people ordinarily talk may in any case turn out to be a two-edged weapon. For there is no doubt that a lot of people do quite regularly derive certain value judgments from certain statements of fact; and this is a feature of their ordinary talk that must receive as much weight as any other in any impartial study.

There are in fact many examples that one could give of this sort of derivation. I may say, to take one possible instance, that I know of a child who is ill, distressed and in pain, likely to die if he does not receive attention but almost certainly curable if he does. These are all straightforward factual assertions; they may, of course, be mistaken or untrue, but they are factual in the important sense that they are open to confirmation or refutation on the normal basis of observation. Not everybody, certainly, would say that if all these assertions were true it would necessarily follow that the parents ought to seek medical help. (Some people, for instance, believe that to do so would be to flout the obvious will of God.) But there are many who would insist that it did follow beyond any doubt—and who might find it impossible to understand what those who disagree could mean when they spoke of 'ought' or 'obligation'.

'Follow beyond any doubt' and similar phrases are, of course, used in ordinary language with a fairly generous degree of imprecision. Sometimes it is used merely in order to express as forcefully as possible a speaker's personal conviction, even though he might readily agree that his convictions could not actually be proved to be correct on the basis of any evidence that he could cite. I have, for example, met people who say that anyone who is a philosopher must obviously be incompetent in the conduct of practical affairs. This conclusion may often be true; but clearly it cannot in any strict sense be said to follow from the premise. It is not part of the meaning of the word 'philosopher' that it should only be applicable to people who are (among other things) incompetent in a practical way; for the deduction to be valid one would need to include as a further premise the empirical generalisation "all philosophers are incompetent"[1]. Somebody might perhaps claim that as far as he was concerned the word 'philosopher' did include as part of its meaning the reference to incompetence, so that for him the generalisation that all philosophers are incompetent would be analytic rather than synthetic. But this would be to use language in a very odd way indeed. It is hard to believe that anyone would be unable to understand the supposition that there should be such a person as a philosopher who is also efficient in a practical manner, however remote he may think the possibility to be. In a similar way many people who would utterly disagree with anyone who said that there was no particular obligation on the parents of the child I described in my example to go to a doctor, would nevertheless be able to understand what he meant. (Failing to understand somebody and disagreeing with him are two completely different things; indeed one must surely understand the meaning of what is said before one can

[1] I am clearly a prejudiced witness, but to the best of my belief this is, as a generalisation, false.

115

know whether one agrees or not.) But, and this is where this case differs from the case of the incompetent philosopher, there are the many others, to whom I referred above, who would be more likely to reply to anyone who suggested that the obligation did not follow from the facts as described, that they were genuinely at a loss to know what he meant when he spoke of obligation. For them, in other words, the obligation follows from the nature of the facts beyond any conceivable doubt, in the proper sense of the word 'conceivable'.

Or suppose, to take a second example of the same sort of situation, that I described somebody as truthful, dependable, helpful, affectionate and so on. Can I after all this sensibly deny that he is a good man? Again there is likely to be disagreement. Some people will certainly say that as to use the word 'good' of anybody is simply to commend him, there is no difficulty in understanding that my outlook might be unusual and the principles on which I base my commendations altogether unlike those of other people. On the other hand, there are the many others who, though they might be able to understand that I could dislike such a man, would regard me as misusing language if I insisted on denying that he was good.

The truth of the matter is that nearly everybody learns to speak and think at very much the same time as they learn about standards, in particular standards of how to behave. In the great majority of cases these standards must inevitably be presented in the first instance as facts, and be accepted as facts. One can certainly hear them repeated as such by one small child to another, both of whom may clearly regard these facts as strange and perhaps disagreeable, but facts nevertheless.

"People oughtn't to take any cake before they've had some bread and butter."

"Why not?"

"Because they oughtn't. That is just how it is."[1]

---

[1] How many grown-ups still feel decidedly guilty if they do not start with bread and butter?

Similarly I can remember hearing a father sadly explaining to his small child that one ought not to put one's elbows on the table, while quite explicitly agreeing that this was a very regrettable fact about the human situation. It is hardly surprising that this early and intimate confusion between values and facts should be reflected in the common use of language.

(It is worth recalling at this point the problem (raised in the last chapter) of the man who relies entirely on the pronouncements of some authority. In practice the securest ascendency that an authority can acquire is precisely to have its values accepted as facts. For facts retain their hold even on people who dislike them. Nearly everyone learns to accept authority before they learn to question it; and some scarcely arrive at the question stage at all.)

Just how intimate is this confusion may be appreciated if we turn back for a moment to my example suggestion about the man who might be truthful, helpful, dependable, affectionate and so on and yet not a good man. The sort of person who would not understand this suggestion is probably the sort of person who might say that 'good' means sometimes one thing and sometimes another[1], and that in such a context as this it simply *means* truthful, dependable, helpful, affectionate, etc.[2] Yet when such a person speaks about someone as good, he will nearly always agree that he is thereby commending the man he is talking about, and not merely describing him in a detached and neutral way. Does this mean that he must suppose that commending is itself one kind of describing? It is possible to argue that this is what his position implies, but on the whole it is not, I think, likely to be what he himself would say. There are much more likely to be certain contexts in which he will very well understand the possibility of neutral description; and others

---

[1] See the beginning of Chapter 2.

[2] It may be that the list should be much longer for the example really to be plausible. But it should not be too hard to imagine how it might be continued.

117

in which he might understand that I was, for instance, commending something without his having any idea of what it was that I was commending. The thing is that there will be other contexts in which, though he may be able to distinguish between commending and describing in the sense that he can see that both are being done, yet he will be unable to see how anyone could withdraw his commendation if he let the description stand; to him it would seem that the description carried the commendation with it. And nearly all the words in the description of my example, 'truthful', 'dependable', and so on, are words which do normally carry with them some degree of commendation. Not that it is by any means impossible to say of someone that he is much too truthful; any more than it is impossible to describe someone as being 'much too good'. But such expressions gain their point through a certain air of sharpened paradox.

It would again be possible to account for this situation in terms of our distinction between criteria and meaning, and say that the description of somebody as truthful, dependable and so on normally carries with it the commendation that it does simply because these characteristics are among our normal criteria for commending people. Not only would it be possible; this is about as clear an account as any one could give. But at the same time it is important to realise that there are contexts in which some people cannot at all understand how it could be possible to talk of separating what we call criteria and meaning. And this brings us back once again to our central problem. For if such people really are unable to understand the possibility of such a separation, what justifies us in saying that there is, at any rate as far as they and their language are concerned, any such separation to be made?

At this stage we seem to have come back to precisely the same point at which we started the chapter, for we are still asking for a justification for the distinction on which so much of the previous argument rests. One thing, however, that does seem to have emerged is the impossibility of

118

maintaining the claim that it rests simply and solely on logic. It is true that if once value judgments can be effectively distinguished from statements of fact, it is then a matter of logic that they can never be deduced from statements of fact alone. But far from there being any pair or group of words the very meanings of which involve the recognition of this distinction (in the way in which the very rules governing the usage of 'all' and 'some' forbid the derivation of a universal statement from a particular), we have seen that if common usage is taken as a guide, there is just as much reason to conclude that the derivation of values from facts is permissible as there is for the opposite conclusion.

So the question now is whether there is any other way in which the distinction can be satisfactorily justified. This is not an easy question to answer; indeed, if I had found it easy I would not have been putting it off for so long. But in the next chapter we must at any rate make some attempt at an answer.

9

'OUGHT' AND 'IS' (ii)—'A RECOGNISABLE DISTINCTION'

THE position we are now in is that I have insisted over and over again that the distinction between value judgments and statements of fact must be regarded as fundamental, but that it seems to be impossible to justify it solely as a matter of logic. Indeed, I have already said about half way through the last chapter that in the last resort we must be content to recognise its existence as a fact of personal experience. At the same time, however, I have admitted that there is something unsatisfactory about this sort of appeal; any independent observer can notice the way you talk, but personal experience is hardly accessible in the same way. And if you maintain that your experience is different from mine, there seems to be little that either of us can do beyond registering our disagreement as a peculiar fact about ourselves alone. But I do not want merely to assert that there seems to me to be a distinction; on the contrary, I should want to maintain that the distinction is one which should be recognised by any normal person.

'Normal' is admittedly a somewhat question-begging word; and there may well be some people who, because of one deficiency or another, will never be able to see any meaning in this distinction between value and fact. But they must be comparatively very rare. The great majority are surely capable of recognising the distinction to some extent or other. The more difficult problem will be to persuade them that the possibility of a separation must *always* in principle be admitted. And this is a matter over which it is worth making some fuss because although there are many for whom this is less a possibility than an obvious and certain assumption, there are many others who would be prepared strenuously to contest it; for example, if not all at any rate an important number of both Marxists and Christians[1].

In one way my position is a very incautious one[2]. For anyone who wished to force me to withdraw would have only to show that there is at least one context in which it is in principle impossible to draw any workable distinction between evaluation and description. But there are some people who are equally incautious in the opposite direction, and who go so far as to argue that there can never be any strictly non-evaluative statement of fact in any context or on any topic whatsoever. They point out, for instance, that to speak of anything at all involves a choice, namely the choice to speak of that thing and not something else, that to pick it out for notice in this way is to attach to it a certain significance and that this is an important form of evaluation. There is, of course, a certain point in this argument. It can sometimes be too easily forgotten that all speech involves some degree of selection, that selection is choice and that many such choices may be in practice very unneutral indeed. And it is true too that it is to a large extent possible to find out what subjects are most important to a man simply by listening to see what he talks about most.

On the other hand there is an absurd side to an argument which suggests that the only way in which one could achieve genuinely neutral statements would be to say everything at once. For it seems obvious that some statements can at the very least be said to be more neutral than others. Suppose, for instance, that I say "Smith weighs precisely 12 stone". I may no doubt have ulterior motives in talking about Smith at all. For perhaps I want to remind you of his existence as a candidate for some job; or I may have chosen

---

[1] I had better make it clear in passing that I do not think that Marxism, still less Christianity, need stand or fall with the acceptance or rejection of this crucial distinction.

[2] It is in fact one which will need a great deal of care to maintain.

I

to talk about his weight rather than about something else, such as his washing habits, that I prefer to leave unmentioned; or again I may be talking about Smith in order to distract your attention from Brown. But whatever my motives may be, it seems clear that they have no bearing upon the truth of my assertion about the amount he weighs, and that whether it is accurate or not will depend solely on the sort of facts which can be established by any properly equipped and independent observer.

Still, we certainly cannot define 'neutral statement' as 'a statement which involves no degree of selection whatsoever'. A better shot at a definition might seem to be 'a statement that is compatible with any expression of *either* approval *or* disapproval of the facts which the statement claims to report'. This would at any rate fit my statement about Smith's weight easily enough. There is no difficulty in understanding that I might either approve or disapprove of his being 12 stone, or, as is more probably the case, that I might not care about the matter one way or the other. And there are, of course, a host of other statements that I might make about him that could equally easily be shown to be neutral in this sense; "Smith is bald", "Smith has only one leg", "Smith has a glass eye", "Smith has ten children". All of these facts about Smith might perfectly well meet either with my approval or disapproval or neither, and all of them are open to straightforward confirmation or refutation by independent observers.

There are other sorts of assertions which might be made about Smith, however, which are not so obviously straightforward. Consider, for example, the assertion that Smith is malicious. It is not perhaps inconceivable that I should approve of his being such a person, but there would undoubtedly be something odd or surprising about it if I did. Certainly, anyone would normally be safe in assuming that I disapproved of him in so far as I believed him to be malicious, unless I made it very clear this was not the case. If I did approve of his maliciousness, this would at the very

least seem to show me to be in conflict with commonly
accepted standards. What is true of 'malicious' is probably
also true, at least as far as ordinary conversation is concerned, of any other terms by which we may describe
someone's character. For it is very hard, if indeed not
actually impossible, to do this without suggesting any
evaluation of him, favourable or otherwise, through the
normal associations of criteria and meaning. There is
nothing very surprising about this. Most people are naturally
so interested in themselves and others as to give any fact
about their ways of behaving a certain relevance to their
standing with each other. And since most evaluations of
such behaviour conform equally naturally to recognised
social stereotypes, it is only to be expected that the same
words should come to carry the description and the
evaluation firmly locked together.

However, the fact that such assertions as "Smith is
malicious" are seldom purely factual or neutral does not
mean it is impossible ever to describe somebody's character
without at the same time evaluating it. In practice what we
need to do is to make up our minds in any context in which
such a description may occur whether we can accept it as
intelligible that anyone should approve, disapprove, or feel
neither one way or the other about what is said. If and in so
far as we can accept all three as equally meaningful
possibilities[1], then we may regard the assertion as a neutral
statement. If, on the other hand, we feel that to describe
Smith as malicious is unavoidably to suggest some disapproval of him, then we may need to look for some alternative
way of referring to what is known about the facts of his
behaviour; a way which would leave it open either to praise
or to blame it or to refrain from doing either.

One way of doing this would be to continue to use the
same terms as before but with a quite explicit declaration
that their evaluative associations were not to be taken into

[1] This does not of course mean that we need to accept them as being
equally probable.

account. In some ways this seems a convenient solution. But it has certain drawbacks. When one is very familiar with one particular use of a word, it is surprisingly difficult to use it consistently in any other however slightly divergent way, even though the decision to do so might originally have been one's own. It is very naturally even harder to be sure that one's listeners or readers will understand and remember as they should one's instructions to ignore customary evaluative associations. This difficulty becomes something very like an impossibility when one takes into account the fact that there is no way of knowing how many people or who may eventually in some indirect or unforeseen way come to hear of a particular discussion. The chances of conveying some evaluation against one's own intentions are all the greater as it is hardly possible to repeat one's disavowals each time any of the crucial words occur throughout a whole long passage, speech or conversation. So there is always a risk of what one says being taken out of its deliberately sterilized context. This incidentally may sometimes be one of the possible justifications for inventing ugly and unfamiliar jargon, which nobody, who is not to some extent familiar with the general context of its use, is likely to understand in any sense at all.

All this goes to show that one needs to be more than careful when trying to adapt ordinary familiar terms to special and unfamiliar uses. All the same, the difficulties of doing this successfully should not be exaggerated into a fatal objection to the possibility of doing it at all. For in the last resort anything that I might say about Smith *could* affect somebody's estimation of him. This is true even of my statement that he weighs exactly 12 stone; for all I know the person to whom I am talking may that very morning have been assured by Smith that he was only 10 st. 8 lbs. and so now be inclined to write him down as a liar. But this has little bearing on my suggested definition of a 'neutral statement'. If it is true that any given statement may in practice affect somebody's evaluation in a particular direction, as it might or might not have been intended to do, this does nothing to show that it is not in theory equally compatible with an evaluation of the opposite sort.

But here once again we return to the same crucial point. For if we wish to insure the neutrality of any statement we may make about somebody's character, or indeed about anything else, by an explicit declaration that any customary associations of approval or disapproval should for these purposes be disregarded, then we need to be able clearly to distinguish what approval and disapproval are. And it must be admitted that probably very few people would be confident of making this distinction in a completely general way, as they might be confident for instance of the distinction between seeing and touching. In these circumstances, there is only one way to proceed with anyone who may be concerned to deny the general validity of our separation between value and fact. We must concentrate first on getting him to recognise it in one particular context; and then, once this basis has been firmly secured, try to move on to extend its application to any other context whatsoever.

The first problem then is to find a context in which the distinction is recognised to be undisputedly clear. It is obviously difficult to be sure of finding just one successful illustration here because of the need to choose different examples according to the interests and experience of whomever it might be with whom one is arguing. But suppose we say, to take one possible instance, that the methods of modern hygiene have reduced infant mortality in many parts of India. Can this be counted as a neutral statement? To some people it might seem that because the word 'mortality' in general and the phrase 'infant mortality' in particular have certain unfavourable associations, the statement that modern hygiene has reduced infant mortality carries with it a strong suggestion of approval for modern hygiene. On the other hand it is often argued that the reduction of infant mortality in a country such as India merely increases an already disastrously over-inflated population, reduces the general standard of living and means that the total number of deaths among somewhat older children as a result of poverty and malnutrition is at least proportionately increased—with, presumably, a corresponding increase in the amount of conscious suffering. Now, perhaps, one no longer knows whether to approve or disapprove the reduction in infant mortality brought about by modern hygiene. We may on the whole be inclined to say that it is in the long run a progressive measure, whose present disagreeable side effects will be removed with the introduction of an effective policy of birth control. But then again, do we approve of birth control? The more one goes into the matter, the more difficult it may become to decide just what one does approve or disapprove of in the whole complicated situation. But whatever conclusion one may come to, whether in the end one finds oneself for or against or still undecided, one thing at any rate remains clear; modern methods of hygiene *have* reduced infant mortality, be it for better or for worse. The fact remains the same whether one approves of it or not.

With other people a more suitable initial example might be found in a discussion of the weather. "It is raining." At some times and in some places it would be so obvious to all concerned whether this news was welcome or not that it would be superfluous to add any further expression of direct approval or disapproval. But it is clearly implicit in this last remark that either of these are equally possible. After a long dry spell, for instance, gardeners will be pleased by rain, but people about to set out on their holidays most probably not. Indeed, somebody who is both a gardener and just about to set out on his holidays will find himself torn between these conflicting considerations. But again the fact remains the fact—it *is* raining. And since this observation is clearly compatible with either approval or disapproval, it follows that neither of them can be deduced from the observation alone. So here at least there can be no denying that a clear distinction exists between factual observation on the one hand and approval or disapproval on the other.

126

The next stage in the argument may seem to consist of a series of restatements of the obvious. Let us suppose that this example about the weather is the one with which we have been working and that it has just been agreed that the observation that it is raining can be accepted as common ground between two people, one of whom approves and the other of whom disapproves of the fact. Anyone who agrees to this must now surely recognise that here at any rate both approval and disapproval are equally attitudes or reactions on the part of the different observers towards the facts on whose nature they agree. Such reactions may be limited to simple feelings of like or dislike, (in which case I would not count them as value judgments); or they may find their place within some quite elaborate system of reasons, principles or purposes. But in either case they are concerned with the ways in which different people may take up positions for or against the facts. It is true, as we have already agreed, that the very noticing of these facts and their registration in the phrase 'it is raining' are also describable as reactions towards them on the part of some observer. But, as should now be clear, these are quite different reactions from those of approval and disapproval, since either of this pair of opposites can be accepted as compatible with the facts as they have been recorded.

We are now in a position to issue a challenge to anyone who nevertheless wishes to deny the possibility of a general application of the distinction that he has accepted as holding in one instance at least. Let him choose any example he likes by which to illustrate his thesis. For the sake of argument we will suppose that he chooses our previous example of the man who is said to be truthful, dependable, helpful, affectionate, etc. These words, we have said, do all normally carry with them some degree of commendation and many people seem to find it impossible to conceive that such a man can seriously be denied to be good. The way to challenge anyone who takes this example might be somewhat as follows. We may first ask him if his use of the word 'good' is here to be understood as conveying commendation or approval (whatever else he may at the same time suppose it to do). He is virtually bound to say yes, since otherwise his example loses its point. Next we ask whether the approval he expresses of the man who is truthful, dependable, and so on, is comparable to the approval he had previously recognised as a reaction or attitude clearly distinguishable from that of describing or reporting. If he answers yes to this, we can point out that as he has recognised that approval is something independent of any particular set of facts, he may transform his hitherto combined account of the truthful and dependable man into a neutral description by explicitly discounting its now admittedly distinguishable element of evaluation. But if he says no, he will find himself in the peculiar position of having two quite different sorts of approval to deal with. We may now finally challenge him to explain what are the relations between them. For either it remains intelligibly open to anyone to approve or disapprove in the independent sense of that other sort of approval, which is said to be tied to certain descriptions or facts; which would be to reduce this second sort of approval to a curiously subordinate position. Or he may claim that the one sort of approval necessarily involves the other; but this would be inconsistent with previous steps in his own argument, as well as with his own admission that the first sort of approval was recognisably independent of any particular facts to which it might be directed.

The last paragraph has, I fear, ended in a tangle. But this is not an accident. On the contrary, a tangle is, it seems to me, where anyone is bound to end who is prepared to recognise in one context the distinction between evaluation and description, but who elsewhere tries to refuse this same recognition. For once the first step is taken, he cannot consistently avoid any of the others. And though it is true that the first step does depend on a simple ability to recognise two sorts of attitudes as different, there are, as I have said, hardly likely to be many people who will not recognise this difference in some context or other, if the point is put to them clearly and forcefully enough. There will indeed be cases in which it will be exceedingly difficult for people of different outlooks and beliefs to agree on a language of common neutrality. For the suspicion that the other man's disavowal of his normal evaluative commitments may, whatever his intentions, be impossible to carry through consistently, is certainly often a reasonable one. But I do not at all wish to argue that it is easy to achieve statements that will be in practice effectively neutral, but merely that to aim at such statements is always intelligible and sometimes highly desirable. In any dispute this is the first and fundamental point of principle on which it is essential to agree; for it is the very condition of rational argument that a common language be established between the persons concerned.

This statement of the case has been, I am only too aware, both too brief and too untidy and there are undoubtedly all sorts of objections that can still be raised. In particular, there are four which may seem extremely powerful and which, successful or not, anyhow raise further points of great interest and importance. To conclude this chapter I shall try and state, but not to answer, these four objections; that I shall try and do in the two chapters that follow.

I might be accused, in the first place, of not having played fair as far as the notion of different sorts of approval is concerned. For after all I had already conceded one chapter ago that even those people who say that a man who is truthful, dependable and so on, must *ipso facto* be good, may still probably understand that I might not like him. But quite apart from this, they will also be familiar with such distinctions as those between moral and aesthetic approval and approval from the point of view of efficiency; and there is no reason why anyone should suppose that the three must always go together. Thus, when somebody says that anyone who is honest, truthful, etc. must necessarily be good, it is obvious enough that this commendation is not

129

intended as one of aesthetic judgment. The best of men from the moral point of view may be hideously ugly and very largely inefficient. What the objector wants to maintain, therefore, may be stated in a more accurate form than I have used so far; namely, that a man who is honest, truthful, etc. is *morally* good, and that anyone denying this merely shows his ignorance, not perhaps of the fact that the word 'good' is used to commend, but certainly of the meaning of moral commendation.

The second possible objection is that it is by no means clear that all value judgments are concerned with either approval or disapproval. For example, I myself have already argued two chapters ago that the word 'true' might best be considered as a value-word, and very much the same might be said of 'probable'—at any rate in non-technical contexts[1]. But I should hardly want to argue that such a sentence as "it is true that there are black swans in Australia" must be taken as indicating the speaker's approval of their presence (or, for that matter, his disapproval). So it looks as if my attempt at a definition of 'neutral statement' would, if taken seriously, make neutral statements of a large number of value judgments. And this seems very odd.

Thirdly, someone might argue that my whole method of argument and in particular my choice of examples have been designed to avoid the really difficult cases. For there are some descriptions, he may say, that are bound up with a whole way of life; there are some facts which cannot be described without thereby taking sides for or against certain ways of behaving. I referred at the beginning of this chapter to the fact that there are some Marxists and some Christians who would want to dispute the claim that the distinction between value and fact is always and unconditionally applicable; and either of them may provide examples of this sort of objection. It

---

[1] As Mr. Hare has pointed out, most sentences in which the word 'probable' ordinarily appears can be retranslated into sentences containing some such phrase as "there is good reason to believe that. . ." in which the presence of the word 'good' brings out the evaluative element quite clearly.

might well be argued, for instance, that there can be no statement of the nature of and relations between the various Christian Churches that is at once complete and neutral, and this for at least two very different sorts of reasons. The first is that there are certain basic essentials which are bound to be differently described by believers and non-believers; for a believer an even approximately satisfactory description of Christ must be almost, if indeed not wholly, at the same time an act of worship, an act in which the non-believer could very obviously not share. The second lies in the very special position claimed by the Roman Catholic Church. The nature of this position and the impossibility of describing it neutrally is shown by the fact that for a Catholic the last few sentences would in strict accuracy have to be written quite differently. For strictly speaking the phrase 'various Christian Churches' can only be used by a Catholic if it is accompanied by very careful qualifications; and for him the *full* and proper statement of the position of his own Church must refer not merely to the claim, but also to the 'fact'[1] that the claim is fully justified. In a not dissimilar way, it is sometimes argued that there can be no neutral description of the position of workers on strike in a capitalist economy, since to attempt to describe it in a detached impersonal manner, as if one had no social commitments, is both anti-Marxist and a way of opting against revolution and for the *status quo*.

The final objection is one which might be said to arise out of all three of the others. It is that in spite of the two examples I have given, the notions of 'approval' and 'disapproval' remain very much too obscure. I have talked of disapproving of the weather. But does this mean merely that it arouses some vague feeling of distaste or must I have reasons for anything I might call approval? Indeed, is approval primarily some sort of inner subjective feeling or is it rather a way of talking and acting? Can one approve

[1] Nor can the decision to put in these inverted commas be any more neutral than would have been a decision to leave them out.

something without being aware one does so? Is it possible to disapprove of something one likes? What is the relation between approving of something and believing it to be important? And so on. None of these questions have obvious straightforward answers; as they certainly should have if the notion of approval is to have a basic role in an argument of the type I have been attempting. In short, 'approval' as I have used it is altogether too wishy-washy a term.

Put like this, these four objections may altogether seem so overwhelming as to over-balance the whole chapter. And indeed, as I have already admitted, they are extremely powerful. I would not, of course, claim anything so absurd as that I could produce a final answer to them all. Nevertheless, I do think that there are answers to be found; and in the following chapters I shall try and make some suggestions as to the directions in which they may lie.

Meanwhile, this chapter may be summed up very briefly. Starting from an acknowledgment that it is impossible to justify the distinction between value judgments and statements of fact solely as a matter of logic, I have attempted to show how this distinction should be regarded not only as fundamental but also as universally applicable. Or any rate applicable by all those who are able in the first instance clearly to recognise it in any one particular context; though with the qualification that the actual elaboration of the distinction may in some cases prove to be a goal to be aimed at rather than something easily and immediately achieved. In developing this argument I was led to throw considerable weight on the notions of 'approval' and 'disapproval'. But among the objections, the very powerful objections, that we have noted, is the one that these notions are far too vague to stand the strain I have placed upon them.

10

'LIKING' AND 'APPROVAL'

OF the objections that I stated at the end of the last chapter, the most sweeping was the fourth. The notions of approval and disapproval are, it was said, far too vague to bear the weight I have placed upon them. There is no denying that there is a good deal in this complaint. And since as well as being the most sweeping, it is also the most fundamental, for I have used the notion of approval at the basic point in the argument, we must spend this chapter in some attempt to meet it and leave the first three objections until we come to the next. We shall not even then, I fear, find ourselves with a sharp and rigorous definition of 'approval'. But, it is worth saying at the outset, we should not be too depressed by the difficulties we may find in the way of providing a satisfactory analysis. Certainly, it is always wise to be as clear as one can be about the terms that one uses. But we need not think that unless we know how to answer all possible questions about either approval or description, we can have no idea at all of how to distinguish between them. After all, to take a similar instance, we may well find it impossible to say exactly what is involved in being bored on the one hand and being interested on the other; but this in no way means that we are always liable to confuse the two.

We may start by considering one of the questions which was raised in the course of the objection; is approval primarily some sort of inner subjective feeling or is it rather a way of talking and acting? The short answer to this question may seem fairly simple, namely it is both. But if we are asked to expand this answer, then the matter becomes very far from simple indeed. What makes it all the more difficult is that 'approval' is in fact a comparatively sophisticated term. Most children learn not only the phrases 'like' and 'don't like', but also indeed the words 'good' and 'bad' long before they come across such words as 'approve' and 'disapprove'. In these circumstances it is usually best to consider the less sophisticated terms first. And since in any case it so happens that another of the questions raised at the same time concerned the relationship between 'approval' and 'liking', we have two good reasons for taking first the parallel question relating to the verb 'to like'. Is to like something a way of feeling or is it rather a way of talking and behaving about it?

At first sight it must seem that if any word refers primarily to individual private experience, this must be the case with the words 'like' and 'dislike'. It is no use anyone telling me that I like marzipan if I know that I do not; in this matter, it seems, I alone am judge. If somebody pesters me enough I may perhaps pretend to like it for the sake of peace and quiet; and if I am pestered a great deal more, I may in the end find it impossible to concentrate enough to be sure whether I still like it or not. But though I may sometimes have to admit to some uncertainty about my own likes and dislikes, at the time of tasting at any rate nobody can ever be more certain about them than I am myself[1].

All this may seem reasonably clear and straightforward until one starts to have second thoughts. But then doubts may arise. There may be complicated doubts such as that about the case of people who have little or no mind of their own and who seem genuinely unable to know whether they like something or not until they are told that they do so. But there may also be much simpler doubts than these. No one takes seriously a child who clamours regularly for chocolate and eats as much of it as he can get, when he protests at the same time that he does not like it. Either, we say, he does not yet understand the meaning of the words

[1] I may, of course, have forgotten whether I like marzipan or not, when somebody else remembers, but this is a somewhat different matter.

he is using or maybe he is pursuing his own form of joke. For it is obvious to everyone that he likes chocolate only too much; one has only to watch his face while he eats it, very probably after he has refused to eat anything else.

This could suggest either that we regard the ways in which he is seen to behave as conclusive evidence of his unseen and unseeable feelings of liking for chocolate; or, perhaps, that the meaning of the phrase "he likes chocolate" lies simply and solely in the way that he asks for it, eats it and protests when there is none, and that it bears no essential reference to any inner feeling at all. There is, surprising though it may seem, a very real temptation to conclude that the second suggestion is the one that is right. There are at least two main reasons for this. In the first place any words that are used by a group of people to communicate with each other have the meanings that they do through the roles that they fulfil in an inter-personal system of language. It is as such that their meanings must be taught and learnt; to learn a new word is to learn how other people use it, and everyone's original understanding of even a word such as 'like' must depend on this basic association with happenings that can be observed not only by himself, but also by those who are teaching him its use. This is part of what is meant when it is said that language is a public or social phenomenon. In the second place any kind of scientific investigation depends essentially on the possibility of observations that can be controlled and repeated by different independent observers. Purely private experience, which is in principle inaccessible to anyone other than the person to whom it occurs, is obviously not open to this sort of control. Some people have in fact argued that there can be no scientific investigation of personal feelings and experience for this very reason. Others, however, regard this attitude as a form of obscurantism, such as science has often had to contend with in the past. They argue rather that feelings, emotions and other such phenomena can perfectly well be understood in terms of publicly observable behaviour and as such are as open to

135

investigation as anything else. (It should be remembered that such behaviour may include not only what can be observed in the ordinary every-day way, but also such things as abnormal glandular activity, which call for much more sophisticated observational techniques.)

Taking these two considerations together, many philosophers have been led to maintain that if one looks into the matter, one will see that the proper usage of terms such as 'like' and 'dislike', as indeed of any other terms, can only be based on such publicly observable criteria. Individuals may undoubtedly associate purely private feelings with their use of particular terms. But this can bear no essential relevance to the rules of meaning which govern their interpersonal use. Indeed, it is doubtful whether such unstable and continually changing phenomena as purely private feelings could be identified as of one sort rather than of another except through their relation to phenomena which *can* be stabilised by public observation and language.

To the ordinary person it must seem preposterous to be suddenly told that a sentence such as "Jimmy likes chocolate" is nothing but a condensed way of referring to certain features of Jimmy's behaviour and only by way of a sort of superfluous accident to any individual feelings or experience that Jimmy might have in the matter. And, of course, it is in a way preposterous. We do all of us, or certainly very nearly all of us, know what it feels like to enjoy or to like something. We know this, as one might say, from the inside; and most people, I imagine, come very quickly to associate the verb 'to like' with a reference to this sort of feeling. Or more accurately, with a reference to a certain typical range of feeling; a feeling of pleasure inseparable from the actual experience of having chocolate in one's mouth, a feeling of regret perhaps when it is finished, a feeling of expectancy when more of it is promised. For when one comes to think of it, a liking for chocolate cannot be one simple unique experience, but is rather something which may manifest itself in a variety of different ways.

For that matter, indeed, most of the time it need not be manifesting itself at all. Even when Jimmy is fully occupied in building sand-castles with no thought of anything else in his mind, it will still be true to say of him that he likes chocolate, meaning by this that when the appropriate situations recur he will normally show and experience the appropriate reactions.

(Although it is not really necessary to do so for the argument of this chapter, this seems a convenient moment to draw attention to another very common piece of philosophical jargon. This is the phrase 'dispositional word'. A word is said to be dispositional when it refers not to any one particular occurrence or set of occurrences, but to a typical though somewhat indefinite selection. For example, if I say that Smith is a smoker, I do not mean that he is smoking now, nor that there are any particular times at which he will be found to be smoking. I mean simply that he smokes fairly often, that he has a tendency or disposition to smoke. 'Smoker' is a simple dispositional word, because it refers to habitual acts of smoking. 'Business-man' might be said to be a complex dispositional term, because there is no one action which could be called 'businessing'; to say that somebody is a business-man is to refer to a whole range of different things that he may usually do. There is perhaps no single thing which all business-men without exception have in common; what they share is a certain typical selection of characteristics. The verb 'to like' may be said, then, to be a dispositional verb. And though there may in this case be identifiable instances of liking or taking pleasure in the actual eating of chocolate, the phrase "he likes chocolate" has a more complex reference than this.)

The fact that as far as most people are concerned to say that Jimmy likes chocolate is primarily a way of referring to feelings which no one but Jimmy experiences, does not, however, mean that the other reference to publicly observable behaviour is altogether lost sight of. For most of the time it is automatically and unthinkingly assumed that the

137

two go together, and puzzles only begin to arise when something suggests that they may have come apart. "He behaves as if he likes chocolate." This familiar way of talking seems to suggest both that there is a discrepancy between his behaviour and his feelings and that what really counts in this matter of liking is not how he is seen to behave, but what he feels 'inside himself'. But why should we suspect that he is only pretending? Do we mean, for instance, that he is never to be found eating chocolate when he thinks himself unobserved? If so, what we are doing is to balance one set of possible or actual observations against another. But suppose that we manage to watch him secretly on a number of occasions and on all of these find him to be eating large quantities of chocolate. Can we still say that perhaps he is only pretending? We might very sensibly say this if we had any reason to believe that he had some special motive for maintaining such an unusually elaborate pretence. Perhaps he has got it into his head that it is of decisive importance for the sake of his social security or prestige to be believed to be a lover of chocolate; and so he takes the extreme precautions of going through all the appropriate motions just in case somebody might be watching, even though he has no particular reason to believe that they are. But again it would naturally be supposed that we should be able to cite some fairly striking instances of eccentric behaviour on his part in support of our suggestion. And if, alternatively, we suggested that his private consumption of chocolate was for the sake of pretending even to himself, it would again be natural to suppose that there must be some other aspects of his behaviour to justify our suspicions; particularly as it becomes peculiarly difficult to distinguish between a consistently successful pretence to oneself and the real thing.

In spite of all this, it may still seem to be an intelligible speculation that somebody might be really pretending, even though there was no point at which one could find any flaw or outward suggestion of pretence. Admittedly, the only way to justify such a speculation would be by reference to some observable word or deed. But, it may be said, it is one thing for a speculation to be unjustified, and quite another for it to be meaningless. It is true that everything he says and does suggests a passion for chocolate; but perhaps underneath he doesn't really like chocolate at all.

It is at this stage of total suspicion, however, that we may begin to see how hard it is to dispense entirely with any reference to the publicly observable behaviour. For now the problem is no longer to know what could justify a reference to some impenetrably private feeling of dislike that might never find any outward manifestation; it is rather how to find out exactly what this reference could mean. The first obvious answers do not seem so obvious when one looks at them twice. For one's instinctive reply that the reference is to the same sort of feelings that one experiences oneself when one has one's own dislikes, lead on to the puzzling question of what possible criterion there could be for the use of the phrase 'same sort'. What basis of comparison could exist between two feelings irretrievably private to two different people? Normally two things are said to be the same when everyone who speaks the same language classifies them in the same way. That is, they are said to be the same with respect to a certain sort of classification; take out this reference to a certain sort of classification and the notion of 'sameness' loses all precision[1]. Public language, however, the language that we all learn, use and teach to our children, can only classify what can be publicly observed. If now we think that to meet this difficulty we can amend our answer to include the necessary public reference by saying that a systematically hidden dislike is a feeling which, *if* it had manifested itself, would have done so in the manner that is accepted as typical, we run into further difficulties. For to be consistent we should presumably have to say that likings also

[1] We cannot describe anything at all without classifying it in one way or another; classification in respect of colour, of shape, of place of origin, of manner of origin, position in space, and so on.

were feelings that showed themselves, when they did so, in certain typical ways. In which case how can we talk of a feeling that has consistently manifested itself as a liking, but which is really a dislike? In practice, of course, this depends on how much evidence is at our disposal. If we have only known somebody for a week, we may very reasonably be suspicious of his consistently manifested liking for us— especially if we possess something which we think he may want. But the case we are concerned with here is that of somebody *all* of whose observable behaviour has *always* been that of a liking. If we have only known him a week, we may suspect that when he gets the chance, that when the moment comes, he may behave very differently. But this is again a reference to behaviour. The odd case, the case that is worrying us, comes if we suppose that his behaviour may *never* show his real feelings.

The truth of this extremely complicated matter is that the normal use of words such as 'like' and 'dislike' refers in some quite unworked out fashion to private feelings and public behaviour at one and the same time. We assume that other people's feelings are essentially similar to our own and that what they say and do is on the whole a fair guide to what they are feeling and thinking; and this assumption seems to work well enough for the ordinary business of understanding and dealing with each other. It may, however, be subjected to various strains and, if the pressure is sufficient, start to break down altogether. Thus, depending on the point from which we start out, we may be led to conclude either that the terms in question refer to inner unobservable feelings alone or, alternatively, only to what is open to outward observation. But neither of these extremes provide in their turn a satisfactory solution. The first makes it very hard to see how we could ever have learnt to communicate meaningfully with each other; but the second though it may in some ways be clearer, departs much too far from the understanding and experience of the people who are, after all, the makers and users of language. For our purposes at any rate we shall do best to stick to the common assumption that when we say that somebody likes something we refer *both* to what he feels *within* and to what we may expect to find him saying and doing; and not expect to be able to lay down any general rule about the proportions in which these two elements are combined.

After this long discussion of the notions of 'like' and 'dislike' considered more or less on their own, we must now turn back to the question of how they are related to 'approval' and 'disapproval'. And the first point to make is that as far as this matter of inner feeling versus outward behaviour is concerned, they are very much on a par. As in the case of liking, to approve of something cannot easily be exclusively identified either with some inward experience or with some range of outward observable behaviour. When we say that somebody approves of something, we normally refer to both of these things at once. The common sense tendency under pressure is, again as in the case of liking, to retreat inwards and to say that in the last resort only the person concerned can know whether he approves of something or not; but this can raise, as before, acute problems of meaning and communication. Both liking and approval are matters of personal attitude; both are dispositions or tendencies to react or behave in an indefinite but typical variety of ways. Above all both are ways of being in favour of something.

So much then for their similarities; what now of the differences between them? As a matter of fact, we have already gone fairly near to discussing this question in Chapter 5[1]. A crude and somewhat distorted way of putting what I said there would be that a value judgment such as might be expressed in the form "X is good", is a liking which could be backed up (or attacked) with reasons based on the nature of X; the straightforward liking is the immediate and unreflecting reaction, and it is in this sense that it may be said to be less sophisticated than approval. The

[1] Pp. 64 ff.

distortion lies in the fact that a value judgment typically makes a much more general claim than an expression or assertion of liking, which is essentially concerned with the personal interests of the speaker. To refer to the earlier discussion, "If I say I like Brown, that is a fact about me. If I say that Brown is a good man and am prepared to support this with reasons, then I claim to say something that will hold good not only for Brown himself but for all others like him in the relevant ways, ways that are referred to in the reasons that I give. At the same time I suggest, what can quite well be the case, that my approval of Brown is wholly independent of my personal feelings of like or dislike towards him, and in this way I claim much more serious attention from other people than I should by a mere expression of private personal feeling."

This passage, and in particular the last sentence, suggests that there is in principle a sharp distinction to be drawn between a commendatory value judgment and an expression of liking; and furthermore that the term 'approval' lies on the value judgment side of the border. There is a great deal of justification for both of these suggestions, but both of them stand in need of certain qualifications. The term 'approval' seems to me in fact to move somewhere between value judgments and expressions of liking, which, as I have suggested earlier, may themselves often be very hard to distinguish in practice. It is not altogether clear, for instance, whether it makes sense to say "although it is bad, I approve of it." Different philosophers at any rate have expressed different views on this point, and it would be curious if this uncertainty were confined to philosophers alone. All the same, 'approval' no doubt remains for most of the time very much closer to the value judgment positions. As to the first point, the distinction between a commendatory value judgment and an expression of liking may become increasingly obscure the more general the nature of the liking expressed. It seems perfectly obvious, at least it seems obvious to me, that we may say things like "although

Jones is a bad lot and I thoroughly disapprove of him, I just can't help liking him"; and conversely we may often dislike people of whom at a distance we approve. But suppose somebody says "I don't like people whose only interest in others is gossip" or "what I want is to see the establishment of a new social order". We have here the expression of a general dislike on the one hand and of a general purpose, or at any rate desire, on the other. And either of these, it seems, might serve as reasons for the justification of individual value judgments.

This last point calls for some expansion. Individual value judgments, we said earlier on, can normally be justified by reference to some more general principle or standard, and this principle may in its turn be justified in terms of another principle more general still. But there is, of course, always a limit to this process of justification in more and more general terms. It is a commonplace of moral philosophy that at the highest level of justification for any given context, at the level that is to say where there are no further reasons to be given for the holding of a principle, one just holds the principle or maintains the purpose, one just approves or has what has been called a pro-attitude. For an objectivist, for someone who thinks that values are some sort of fact, this situation gives rise to no particular difficulty. But it may well seem that on the view I have been putting forward it must mean that at the highest level the assertion of principle becomes after all an assertion or expression of personal fact; that, for example, there remains only a verbal difference between "the happiness of others is the ultimate justification" and "there is nothing which in the long run gives me greater overall satisfaction to promote or to contemplate than the happiness of others". Sometimes no doubt this is in effect the case. But the situation is probably seldom as simple as that.

The most obvious prima facie difference between the two formulations is that the first purports to lay down a standard, while the second may be a personal claim or confession.

(There is also the difference that as a claim it may seem decidedly smug.) What does one mean here by talking of 'laying down a standard'? One thing one means is that by so doing reasons or justifications may be provided for all sorts of particular value judgments, actions or efforts. To lay down a standard is, usually at any rate, to make a *social* claim; it is to claim other people's allegiance to the standard and their disapproval of those who deliberately reject it. The reasons it will supply for particular value judgments are claimed as reasons why anyone else should make the same value judgments. None of these things are claimed by a mere assertion of liking, however general it may be. So far, so good. But there are some contexts in which the claim of the standard may be very much weaker than in others, and some in which it may even be possible to renounce it altogether. For suppose somebody says, for example, "as far as I am concerned, the happiness of others is the ultimate justification", meaning thereby that this is the standard by which he tries to act and by which he evaluates his own successes and failures. Does this commit him to condemning you in so far as you act on some other basis? At any rate, if he felt that such a commitment might be involved, he could restate his personal standard in terms of an over-riding purpose without entangling himself in suggested evaluations of anyone else; "I intend always to try and act in such a way as to further where possible the happiness of others." If you do not altogether share such wishes, if perhaps you put service to some other cause above human happiness, you presumably will not always try to do the same sorts of things that he does. But that is all; you are different and you have a different outlook. He has a standard by which he may evaluate his own actions as good or bad, successful or unsuccessful, consistent or inconsistent, as the case may be; but his standard is one by which he will not judge anybody else.

Thus there are points at which value judgments of approval or disapproval on the one hand and expressions of like or dislike on the other come very close to each other. Both are ways of being for or against somebody or something. The main differences between them seem to be that value judgments are connected with reasons and general principles, while likes and dislikes may stand on their own; and that value judgments are, or claim to be, detached from personal interests and feelings in a way in which likes and dislikes very obviously are not. These are very important differences, but they are all the same differences that may overlap. Many likes and dislikes are in fact supported by reasons, and some people's principles of evaluation have no application to any but their own actions and efforts. Moreover, the fact that likings and approvals are both generally to be understood not as single experiences of some pure and uniquely identifiable type, but rather as dispositions to feel and behave in a variety of more or less loosely related ways, makes it even more impossible to draw one sharp boundary line between them. Approvals are more detached; this may suggest that feelings of any sort enter into them very much less than they do into likings. But once again it is impossible to form any simple generalisation. People may feel intensely about their general principles; and some likings may be very tepid indeed.

And how, it may be asked, does all this leave the question whether it is possible to disapprove of something one likes? In point of fact, of course, I have already answered this question only four or five paragraphs ago, when I said that I found it obviously possible to like a man of whom I thoroughly disapproved. And in spite of what I have just said about the difficulty of making a sharp general distinction between liking and approval, this still seems to me as obvious as it did before. It is very natural for people to be at the same time for or against the same person or thing from a number of different points of view. And once again the fact that there may sometimes be cases where, because of conflicting criteria, we do not know exactly how to apply a distinction, does not mean that there are not many more cases where the distinction is perfectly clear. So, for example, I may enjoy a man's company, find him amusing and charming, be glad to see him come and sorry when he goes—in short I like him; on the other hand he is undoubtedly self-centred and unscrupulous, and with a powerful influence over other people which he uses without the least concern for their happiness—hence I disapprove of him. I may be forced perhaps to agree that I ought not to like him; but there it is, I do. Quite different from his tedious and self-sacrificing neighbour, whose heart is in all the right places, but who has less than no sense of humour and whose unceasing preoccupation with the misery of the world is a constant and maddening accusation of one's own comparative frivolity.

In any case whatever difficulties there may be in the way of providing an exact analysis of what it is to approve and of distinguishing approving from liking, the essential point is that both are ways of being for something, forms of favour or welcome. Some simple people, simple not in the sense of 'silly' but in the sense of being 'all of one piece', may be incapable of having different and conflicting reactions towards something at one and the same time. But not everybody is like this; and neither approval nor liking are necessarily exclusive of simultaneous reactions of disfavour or hostility to the same thing considered from other points of view. Both, however, are recognisably different from the record or description that is a statement of fact. And if I claim, as I have done, that we know nearly all of us what it is to approve, there is some advantage in the natural vagueness of the term. For we may know what it is to be for or in favour of something, even if we are not too sure of how to distinguish one sort of pro-attitude from another.

All the same, it will be safer now slightly to modify my provisional definition of 'a neutral statement' of a chapter ago to "a statement that is compatible with any expression of *either* being for *or* being against the facts which the statement claims to report". This formula is not, I fear, very

146

neat, but it will perhaps serve its purpose. It is true that evaluations are not the only form of pro- or con-attitude that are thereby ruled out as unneutral. But there has, of course, never been any suggestion that all assertions which are not neutral statements, are therefore value judgments.

The whole of this chapter has arisen out of the objection that my use of the notions of approval and disapproval had hitherto been much too vague. I am not at all sure that I have in fact done very much to make them noticeably less so. (Nor have I provided answers even to all of the questions that I myself mentioned). But what I have tried to do is to show what sort of notions they are, and in particular some of the ways in which they are related to those of like and dislike. All of these are typically dispositional terms. That is to say that though people may sometimes have particular experiences or feelings which they might describe as feelings of liking or approval, to like or to approve of somebody or something is not merely a matter of having these feelings. It is rather a disposition or tendency to experience a certain range of feelings as well as to talk and behave in a variety of recognisably typical ways. In particular we referred to the difficult and puzzling matter of the impossibility of identifying likings or approvals with either inner feelings or outwardly observable behaviour to the exclusion of the other. Finally we noted that although there are a number of criteria by which it is normally possible to distinguish between liking and approval, there are certain border-line cases on which to impose the distinction would involve a more or less arbitrary decision. But none of these uncertainties seriously affect my attempt at definition of 'a neutral statement'. For both approval and liking involve an experience of being in one way or another for or in favour of something; and this experience, I have claimed, is recognisably different from the effort to describe or report what that something is.

11

THE MEANING OF 'MORAL', OF 'VALUE-JUDGMENT' AND OF 'NEUTRAL STATEMENT'

(i)

IN THE last chapter I have attempted to deal with the fourth and most comprehensive of the objections I listed in the chapter previous to that. In this one we may go back and take the other three in their original order. The first of these, you will remember, focussed attention specifically on the question of moral value judgments, where previously we had been talking of value judgments in general. It was that of the man who is willing to concede some sense in which I might dislike or disapprove of someone who, to stick to our previous example, is honest, truthful, dependable and so on; but who maintains that if I pretend that such a man is not *morally* good, I merely show my own ignorance of the meaning of moral commendation. Since this is meant to be a book on moral philosophy, we should in any case be bound at some point or another to say something about the family of terms associated with 'morality'. And this objection gives us a good opportunity.

The word 'moral' is derived from the Latin 'mores', and the *mores* of a community are its customs, its accepted ways of behaviour as a community. The etymology of a word is, of course, by no means always any great use as a guide towards its present meaning. But 'moral' has on the whole remained in pretty close contact with its origins. By and large we use the phrase 'moral principles' for those principles which regulate our conduct towards society, and 'moral questions' for those which concern our relations with other people considered as members of the wider or narrower community to which we belong. If we could add that the term was used exclusively to refer to those principles which are not only about social behaviour, but which are in fact the socially recognised standards governing such behaviour, the matter would be reasonably straightforward. For it would then be possible to use the words 'moral' and 'immoral' simply to describe behaviour as either in accordance with accepted standards or not, without necessarily implying thereby either approval or disapproval of the individual or the community. But though these words may sometimes be used in this way, they are not always so. It is probably more usual for them to perform an evaluative as well as a descriptive function.

'Moral' has, it seems to me, two main evaluative functions, distinct from and not altogether compatible with each other. In the first place it is frequently used by someone in application of his own standards of social behaviour, his own view of how man should behave to man. That is to say that it is used like 'good' as a commendatory or approving term. But where 'good' is a quite general term of commendation, the use of 'moral' indicates a certain context or point of view from which whatever it may be is being judged, namely the context of social behaviour. Again, if this were the only use of the term, the matter would be comparatively straightforward. We should know whenever anybody used it that he was doing so to express a favourable value judgment of a certain specific kind. However, as well as the descriptive use of 'moral' that was mentioned above, there is another way to be considered in which it may be used to express a value judgment. For it is also sometimes used to indicate that the aspect of the situation under judgment is of overriding importance. For example, "The moral duty of an artist is to put his art before everything, if necessary even before his duty to himself and to his fellow men". My moral duty (in this sense) is the duty that really matters, the duty which I must in the last resort put first. And, depending on the situation and on the point of view being expressed, may or may not be my duty to my fellow members of society. I know people who feel that the first and most important thing to decide when they are faced with a practical problem is whether there are any moral issues involved. They may, of course, mean only that the first thing to do is to discover whether as a matter of fact there are any issues involved concerning principles of social behaviour. But I think that at least part of what they mean is rather that the first thing to do is to make up one's mind whether or not the issues involved, whatever they may be, should be regarded as of fundamental importance.

The main difficulties and misunderstandings to which different uses of the word 'moral' may give rise are due to the fact that it quite commonly performs each of the three functions that I have just distinguished. For some people all three may go together—people who fully accept, so fully perhaps that the acceptance is not even a conscious one, the socially accepted standards of behaviour as their own, and who regard the obligations they impose and the values they embody as more important than any other. Others may agree that the most important principles are those which govern social behaviour, but deliberately reject the currently accepted standards as immoral. Or, they may express precisely the same point of view by explicitly disapproving of much 'moral behaviour', if they are more accustomed to using the word in its descriptive sense to indicate behaviour of which the community would approve. Other people again may accept community standards as far as they go with the important reservation that they are not prepared to consider moral standards in this sense of 'moral' as necessarily and in every situation more important than any other. And so on. There are other ways in which the various possibilities may be combined. And what may add to the confusion is that very often one and the same person will slide from one usage to another without noticing that he has done so. Indeed, in the unreflecting course of a great deal of common speech the running together of two or more of the various alternatives may be less the exception than the rule.

How then are we to understand the objection that someone who is honest, truthful, dependable, etc. is *ipso facto* morally commendable? As far as the main descriptive use of the word 'moral' is concerned, it is no doubt the case that such a man would receive high approval in accordance with the standards that are accepted and taught by a large majority of the community. But to say that somebody is morally good in this sense is simply to report on the qualities that he has and on how they would generally be judged, and not in itself to express any approval of either qualities or judgment. No doubt many people take their moral standards from the community, learning them as facts and operating them as standards without ever really noticing that these are two different things. But we have seen how hard it is not to recognise some sort of distinction between description and evaluation, when attention is called to it in the appropriate way. Thus the particular objection we are considering here actually starts from the concession that there may always be some sense in which I might dislike or disapprove of anyone, whatever his qualities might be. The word 'moral', however, helps to tie evaluation and description back to each other again, because, unlike 'good' standing on its own, it also has this specific descriptive function. This is what makes it so much easier to slip backwards and forwards between evaluation and description in the judgment that somebody who would be regarded by the community as morally good, *is* morally good.

All the same, nobody is logically compelled to accept, endorse or approve the standards of the community in which he finds himself, hard though it may be for many people not in fact to do so. If the term 'moral' is understood in a purely descriptive sense and if 'moral commendation' means simply 'commendation from the point of view of what is generally approved', then what is asserted by the objection may be true without being an objection. For honesty, truthfulness, dependability and so on may be generally approved as forms of social behaviour, and to say that they are so merely to point out a straightforward matter of fact. What if 'moral' is used to refer to any principles concerned with social behaviour whether they conform to current social standards or not? It may perhaps be argued that no society could survive in which such virtues as honesty and truthfulness were not actively encouraged, and hence that they are among the conditions necessary for the maintenance of any moral principles whatsoever— for if morals are about social behaviour, without society there can be no morals, But even if this argument is accepted[1], there would still be no logically compelling reasons why anyone should approve of these qualities. For I may disapprove both of the existence of organised society and of anyone who either supports or succumbs to its pressures; I may approve only of individual ruthlessness and resource and the will to get the best of other people by all possible means, and not at all of what I might regard as feeble-minded surrenders to social convention. And unless I myself share some standpoint which could be called 'moral' in the sense of concern with social behaviour, my recognition that certain qualities are commendable from a moral standpoint may not necessarily lead *me* to commend them.

How unlikely this supposition might be may be open to some argument. Most people do in fact probably approve from a moral standpoint of the sort of qualities mentioned, in at any rate one of the various possible senses or combination of senses of 'moral'. But though it may also be true that for perhaps a majority of them the very meaning of the phrase 'moral commendation' does commit them to the approval of certain specific forms of behaviour, this meaning must be one in which two quite different elements are combined and confused; elements which it is not easy but

[1] In point of fact it would have to be hedged in by a very great number of qualifications if it were to have any chance of standing up to a well-informed attack.

nevertheless possible to distinguish as a result of careful enough analysis.

There are, of course, a large number of other things that might be asked or said about the term 'moral' and its related family. What, for example, is the exact nature of the relation between morality and freedom? It is often claimed that it is part of the very meaning of 'moral' that moral judgments can be made only of actions and behaviour under voluntary control. But is this really so? And if it is so, why? Then again, there is the famous question as to whether we can have moral duties towards animals. There is the question whether one can have moral duties to one-self. There is the question whether *all* social actions should be considered to have moral implications and if not, why not?[1] And there are other similar questions. But it will be impossible to discuss any of them clearly without first making up one's mind as to which of the senses distinguished above should be given to the key word. Have we moral duties towards animals? This could be treated as a question about the degree of importance one should attach to our treatment of animals in comparison with our treatment of our fellow human beings. It might be a question about whether animals should be considered as forming part of society; and this, though similar to the last question, is not entirely the same, and involves too some further consideration of the complex notion of 'society'. Or it might perhaps be treated as a purely factual question about social habits, the sort of question that might be answered with the information that the English do recognize such duties, but that hardly anybody else does. Happily, however, these are matters that do not directly concern the point under immediate discussion. For the present it is enough to note

[1] What is the difference, for instance, between rules of morality and rules of politeness? There is here an interesting link between the two evaluative functions of 'moral' in so far as the most plausible short answer may seem to be that moral actions are those which are of the greatest importance. (To some people, of course, politeness may anyhow be itself a moral duty.)

153

L

that 'moral' is a word whose descriptive and evaluative functions are peculiarly closely intertwined, but which can nevertheless be sorted out if one has the time and patience.

(ii)

The second objection raises an equally important point, though one of a very different kind. Essentially it concerns the use of the phrase 'value judgment', and arose out of my first attempt at definition of the phrase 'neutral statement' in terms of approval and disapproval. For, as I put the objection, "it is by no means clear that all value judgments are concerned with either approval or disapproval . . . it looks as if my attempt at a definition of 'neutral statement' would, if taken seriously make neutral statements of a large number of value judgments. And this seems very odd." This objection can no longer be put in exactly the same way in view of the modified definition which I produced at the end of the last chapter, and according to which 'neutral statement' can now be regarded as "a statement that is compatible with any expression of *either* being for *or* being against the facts which the statement claims to report". But it has still to be admitted that although I have argued that 'true' may best be considered as a value-word, I should not at all want to maintain that my assertion that "it is true that there are black swans in Australia" involves my being for or against their presence there.

As a matter of fact this objection might have been put very much more fiercely. For if 'true' is a value word, then presumably I am bound to argue in parallel fashion that an assertion beginning "it is true that . . ." is a value judgment. But at the same time it would seem preposterous to suggest that an assertion such as "it is true that there are black swans in Australia" is anything other than a statement of fact. Indeed, in Chapter 5 I went out of my way to remark on the close links between the terms 'true' and 'fact'. So if

154

I want to maintain both these theses, how can I possibly continue to defend the universality of my distinction between value judgments and statements of fact?

There is clearly no point in my trying to turn aside this objection without having to admit any modification in the various positions that I have so far taken up. I cannot consistently have it both ways at once. When I explained in Chapter 8 that the doctrine that an 'ought' can never be derived from an 'is' cannot be taken literally, I suggested that a better formulation might be that no value judgment can be derived from a statement of fact. But if I wish to account for the various ways in which the word 'true' is used by describing it as a value-word, I shall clearly have to look for yet another formulation for the doctrine about 'ought' and 'is'. If, on the other hand, I wish to stick to the formulation which I have been using so far, and which is pretty widely accepted, I shall have to refashion my suggested solution of the problems raised by the word 'true'. And I might as well admit before going further that I am not entirely sure which of the alternatives is preferable[1].

But how exactly have we got into this not very satis-factory position? In a way it is due to my never having made any attempt at a formal and rigorous definition of the phrase 'value judgment' (though I did point out in Chapter 5 that to stipulate that value judgments must always be backable with reasons, is a move in that direction). Instead, I have been using 'value judgment' and its related terms on the assumption that the context would make their use sufficiently intelligible. It is undeniably very risky to intro-duce and use one's key terms in this free and easy sort of way, and a confusion such as the one we are faced with at

---

[1] It might seem that I could at a technical pinch argue that the assertion "It is true that there are black swans in Australia" is not itself a statement of fact, but rather a value judgment about one. Just how makeshift or implausible an expedient this would be, I am not quite sure; but it is not worth arguing here as the assertion in question can in any case be in its turn derived from what is beyond doubt a statement of fact, namely the assertion "There are black swans in Australia".

155

present is often the result. On the other hand, a rigorous definition of a key term in a complicated analysis often involves some fairly technical considerations. Even if it were possible to present such a definition at the very beginning, it would be hard for anyone who had not already seen what sort of analysis the subject matter called for, to remember exactly what the definition was, let alone to understand it. For one obviously cannot know how to formulate such definitions until one has seen the points at which loose familiar usages break down. The present confusion is one of these, and we must now try to do something to show how it might be cleared up. But I shall still not feel in a position to attempt a formal definition of 'value judgment'. Indeed, such a definition is considerably beyond my ambitions in this book; for the present it must remain one of those problems which are raised only to be left over for further consideration.

The immediate question before us is whether or not 'evaluation' should be necessarily linked with 'approval' or 'disapproval'. On the whole this does seem to be the most natural thing to do. There are many common associations between the notions of value and of rating higher or lower in a scale of approval or importance. In particular, the question with which we embarked on this whole enquiry was that of the meaning of 'good'; and this word is most typically used precisely to signify approval or commendation. How then did we slip into using the term 'value-word' in our analysis of 'true'? The reason was because we found that we could give the neatest account of this word in terms of the distinction between meaning and criteria, which we had already used for the analysis of 'good'; because 'true' provides no particular descriptive information about anything, but is used rather to affirm or confirm on the basis of criteria that differ in different contexts; and because these notions of affirmation and confirmation seem to belong to the same family as those of approval and disapproval. They both involve forms of appraisal or appreciation—'appreciation' in the sense of estimating a situation, without necessarily estimating it favourably.

All the same, it may well seem that the association between evaluation and approval is the most important of all these conflicting considerations. For throughout the argument of the last four chapters the basis for my contention that no value judgment can be derived from any statement of fact, has been that nearly everybody can recognise a difference between being for or against something on the one hand, and merely trying on the other hand to discover and report what that something is. It is one thing, as I have kept on arguing, to take note of a situation and another to react towards that situation favourably or unfavourably; if the two often go together in practice, they are in principle at any rate different and distinguishable. And since this distinction is fundamental in its turn to the main argument of this book, it seems as if anything odd there might be about the idea of neutral value judgments must come not so much from my account of neutrality as from the over-free way in which I used the term 'value judgment' in the earlier chapter.

So it looks as if the simplest way out would be to jettison my account of the meaning of 'true', and restrict the use of 'value judgment' to assertions which embody some expression of being for or against, and which can be backed-up with reasons. (And perhaps more besides, when we come to a fully-fledged definition.) Jettisoning is certainly a simple enough operation. The trouble is that a replacement would then have to be found; and anyhow I think that there is a good deal to be said for my present account of 'true'. Moreover, it should after all be possible to preserve its substance with a little more care over the use of such terms as 'value-word', 'value judgment' and the rest. One possible course would be to say not that 'true' *is* a value-word, but that it is in many ways like one, pointing out as before the specific forms of resemblance. Alternatively, I might keep the wider use of 'value judgment', and reformulate the distinction upon which my main argument is based in terms of a restricted class of value judgments only. On the whole I am inclined to think that this would be a clumsy solution. But for the present perhaps I may be excused from having finally to make up my mind. It is better to state a problem as clearly as one can and to leave it at that rather than to force a solution before one is ready.

Meanwhile, we may sum up this section by saying that though the objection does nothing, and indeed claimed to do nothing, against my distinction between approval and description as such, it has brought out into the open a serious underlying inconsistency in my use of the family of terms clustered around 'value judgment'. And this is beyond doubt a very important thing to have done.

(iii)

The third objection related to statements and descriptions which seem to form an integral part of some very general outlook or world-view. The argument was that in certain cases the very way in which facts may be described may be inseparably bound up with a certain attitude towards them, and that there is therefore no neutral way of reporting such facts. This objection is particularly difficult to discuss properly without presenting a fully worked-out example. But since such an example would in the nature of the case involve the presentation of some elaborate and far-reaching theory or set of beliefs, to try and do it as it should be done might well turn out to need the best part of a book of its own, and so is not something that we could possibly try and do here. Happily, however, this should not matter quite as much as it might have done; for once again I shall not try to repel the objection head-on. On the contrary, the main point on which it it based is both sound and important. What I hope to show is that it is not after all inconsistent with my position.

"A neutral statement", according to my rough definition

"is a statement that is compatible with any expression of either being for or against the facts which the statement claims to report." One cannot make statements without using language and one may, of course, make them honestly or dishonestly and from a wide variety of motives. My definition has fairly clearly nothing to do with the intentions or the unintentional effects which anyone who utters a statement may either have or bring about; or, to put the matter a little more accurately, a statement may be neutral in accordance with this definition although uttered with most partisan intentions. So the definition makes no pretence to provide some criterion of absolute neutrality (whatever that might be), which would apply not only to what statements mean, but at the same time to every other aspect of the contexts in which they might be used. There is no doubt that such a simple and straightforward assertion as "there is a strong smell in this room" may in certain circumstances both carry and evoke the strongest feelings of approval or hostility; but this is not relevant as far as its meaning is concerned, since it would be equally compatible with either.

Statements, then, are inseparably bound to language. And I should agree straight away that some languages, or at any rate some aspects of them, are in their turn hardly separable from certain very definite orientations. The examples that we took earlier on to illustrate this objection (examples referring to certain Christian and Marxist ways of talking) are good examples. They can, I think, successfully be used to show how to describe the facts in one way may very naturally provide reasons for one set of attitudes towards them, while the alternative description may be associated with principles on which an opposing outlook is based. So I am not trying to suggest that there is or could be any absolutely neutral language, based perhaps on some absolutely neutral world-outlook. I have, on the other hand, claimed that nearly everyone is capable of recognising the distinction between description and evaluation if the matter is put to them clearly enough; and this means everyone whatever their world-outlook may be. So, whether they use one form of description or another, they should be able to distinguish and explicitly disavow the elements of approval or disapproval that there may be in any of what they take to be statements of fact. And so it would seem to follow that a neutral statement need not necessarily be neutral as *between* two languages or outlooks, but neutral with respect to or *within* one language or the other.

This probably seems a very obscure thing to say. It may help to make it a bit clearer if we expand for a little way one of our two previous examples. Let us suppose that in trying to explain the nature of a series of strikes, a Marxist says among other things that "the last year or so has seen a definite sharpening of the class struggle". This typically Marxist phrase 'class struggle' cannot easily be explained in a sentence or two. Indeed, part of the point of the example lies in the fact that it can really only be understood against the whole complex background of Marxist theory about the nature of social classes and the working of history, politics and economics, in short society. As a matter of fact, it is even then possible to find one Marxist disputing with another the precise meaning to be given to 'class'. For Marxism is less one specific theory than a very general framework in which it is possible to formulate a considerable variety of more specific views. All the same such views belong to the one family; and merely to describe the situation in terms of class struggle is already to some extent to take sides in a conflict that has not only intellectual, but also political and social implications. For somebody of more conservative or 'right wing' views is naturally much more inclined to think in terms of the nation as one whole. As far as he is concerned, to describe a situation in terms of class struggle at all is already to beg the question, to incite people to imagine themselves divided where what they should see is really their essential unity. So he would want to start by describing whatever facts may lie behind the reference to class struggle in some quite different and, from his standpoint, non-tendentious way. Whereas for the Marxist the only accurate description would be as in the example, and the tendentious one that which attempted to bemuse people with a pretended unity in order to conceal from them their basic divisions.

One might ask, of course, why one should talk of unity or divisions at all. Why not just say that certain workers are on strike? Surely, this is a statement on which both Marxist and non-Marxist could agree. So indeed it is. But it is only a statement and no sort of explanation. Moreover, from a Marxist standpoint to refuse to describe the situation as a whole is to distort the nature of each part of the situation taken on its own; it is to conceal the possible implications for action that its various aspects may have when seen in relation to each other. A strike is not just a strike, a purely local affair. It is a way of reacting to a complex social situation, and can only properly be understood within the context in which it arises.

In spite of all this, however, few Marxists would want to deny that capitalists might disapprove of those facts of which a Marxist approves. Quite the contrary. It is true that Marxists may believe that the average capitalist is unlikely to be able to attain a clear view of the facts, handicapped as he is by the distorted outlook on the world with which they think he has grown up. But essentially their position, or at any rate that of a great many of them, is not that a true understanding of the facts must necessarily lead everyone who understands to rejoice; but rather that though one may either approve or disapprove depending largely on one's own social situation, one cannot get out of doing either of these.

As a purely practical matter there are times when this argument may have considerable point. In periods of conflict there may be good sense in the old slogan "All those who are not for us are against us", and there are occasions when the claim that it is possible to take an impartial view of the facts may actually do considerable damage to one side or the other. But if and when this is so, it is because of the ways in

161

which other people may react to such an example of neutrality. To put it paradoxically, there are times when an impartial study may be an important weapon in the hands of one side or the other. But this does not mean that the study itself may not be quite impartial or neutral in being restricted to the facts alone. Indeed, if it is allowed that different people may either approve or disapprove of one and the same set of facts, it clearly follows that the facts cannot be inseparable from either of these reactions. And if both are thus recognisably separable, then it seems equally clear that it must be possible to separate them and to consider the fact as a fact alone. To deny this for any length of time is effectively to abandon the possibility of clear and independent thinking; which is a point that many Marxists are themselves beginning to realise.

The upshot of this is that a Marxist who is able in any one context to distinguish between approval and description, should thereafter be able to seek ways of divorcing the evaluative from the purely descriptive elements of his language whatever subjects he may discuss. In other words a Marxist is here in exactly the same position as anyone else. Once he has recognised the crucial distinction, he can no more validly derive a value judgment from a statement of fact within his framework of description than can the capitalist or bourgeois within his. Both of them, within their respective languages, will be able to form neutral statements. The only thing is that the statements will not be the same. For nobody could construct a language which would be neutral between all possible points of view. The capitalist will still have his way of describing certain situations and the Marxist another. If both sides can agree, however, to set aside questions of approval, it then becomes possible to consider the rival ways of presenting the facts on their own factual merits. Clarity of this sort is the first step towards profitable discussion. Subsequently it may be possible to adjust the rival languages and systems of thought to each other precisely by concentrating on the purely factual elements within them, and where possible on ways of testing and retesting these facts and the theories on which their description is based. Even if people come to speak the same language and to share the same general outlook, this would not of course necessarily mean they would all agree about everything. But it would be often[1] worthwhile at least to speak the same language.

It is worth noting that even if by the conscientious exclusion of both approval and disapproval agreement was eventually reached on one system of description or another and on a common outlook, this would still be one possible outlook among others. It would not be neutral in any absolute sense, because there is no sense in the idea of absolute neutrality. It would be incompatible, for instance, with outlooks which were embedded in what were now seen as unsatisfactory modes of description. The truth is not neutral against false beliefs.

So the most important result of this objection has been to clarify my notion of neutrality. It is true that some descriptions are inseparable from one outlook rather than another; it is true that there are some facts that one cannot describe without taking sides. But the distinction between approval and description will hold, if not between languages, yet within any language whatsoever. And one of the necessary conditions for successful communication between people of different outlooks is for each of them to see that within their respective languages this distinction is preserved.

(iv)

On top of these four objections there is one further point which calls for some discussion by way of a postscript. We have already noted the potentially ambiguous nature of

---

[1] It would be pleasant to be able to take the optimistic and rationalistic step of exchanging this 'often' for 'always'. But it has to be admitted that people may sometimes get on very much better if they do not always understand what each other's outlook is.

sentences such as "I approve of X". These are sentences which look like statements of fact about the speaker, but which can usually be better understood as expressions of approval towards X or whatever it may be. Words like 'approve' are sometimes called performatory words; that is to say that, when used in the first person, they form an integral part of some verbal action. When I say, for example, "I promise to be faithful", I am not describing what I am doing, or stating that I am making a promise; to say 'I promise' is an important part of promising. In the same way, to say "I approve of X" is very often simply a way of expressing that approval. But it would be silly to try and insist that this is always how it must be interpreted; for it is quite natural that we should sometimes want to inform somebody else of the nature of our standards as a fact about our own outlook. Somebody may ask me, perhaps, about what principles I hold and I may reply by saying "Well, for instance, I approve of X"; and though my assertion may well be taken as at the same time expressing my approval for X, it would be quite implausible to say in such a context that it was not for that reason a statement.

It is those occasions on which it is obvious that a sentence such as "I approve of X" must be treated as a statement, that raise the problem. It is true, clearly, that the fact that I approve is no sufficient reason why anyone else should approve too. But it does seem that as far as the speaker is concerned the statement "I approve of X" commits him to saying that X is good. In other words he cannot consistently assert the statement while withholding the value judgment. And here once again would seem to be an exception to the general rule that I have been trying so hard to defend that there is always a fundamental distinction between the two. To put it another way, the fact that I approve of X involves my approval of X; the value is inescapably derivable from the fact.

This objection is rather different from the other four, in that it is an essentially technical one. This is not to say that the other objections involve no technicalities; but rather that statements about one's own principles and values constitute a very special and limited class, and the considerations which make of them apparent exceptions to the rule are strictly peculiar to them alone. However, this does not make the matter any less important. Exceptions are exceptions; and, if they are genuine, one should not in philosophy try to get away with it by claiming that they prove the rule. On the contrary, the rule would be definitely discredited. However, though the matter is complicated I do not think that it is as bad as it may seem.

The point of the doctrine about the separation of fact and value is that there can be no proper move from an assertion of fact to an evaluation of the fact that is asserted. It is the last clause that is important here. The statement "I approve of X" is a statement about myself; but the value judgment to which it seems to commit me is a value judgment about X. All the previous objections have been concerned with the possibility of finding some assertion in which a description and an evaluation of one and the same thing were inseparably combined. But here the assertion is about me and the value judgment is not. So although in a way this is undeniably a case of a value judgment that is derivable from a statement of fact, it is not the sort of case whose possibility I have been trying so hard to deny.

Somebody might say, however, that my assertion that I approve of X commits me not only to an approval of X, but also to approving of myself for approving. This suggestion would indeed provide a genuine exception to the rule in that the value judgment would be about the same thing as the statement, i.e. my approval of X. At least, an exception would be provided if the suggestion made sense, but it doesn't. It is true that I can disapprove of or possibly dislike myself for *liking*, for example, gambling. But this is one of the points at which a liking is essentially different from a value judgment of approval. For a value judgment necessarily involves reasons. So if I approve of gambling or anything else, this means that I must have reasons for doing so. I may also perhaps have other and different reasons for disapproving of gambling from some other point of view; considerations do often conflict like this. But I cannot at one and the same time have reasons for approval and reasons for disapproval of those very same reasons. For this would cancel out. And if I cannot disapprove of myself for approving something, then to approve of myself for so doing would be equally superfluous. There is no standpoint from which I can approve of my own approvals.

But this argument is not altogether finished even yet. The statement "I approve of X" is a statement about myself; but what about the statement "X is the sort of thing about which I approve"? This does seem to be a statement about X itself, and it too must commit me to a favourable evaluation of X. Now, it is undeniable that I can classify objects I under such headings as (i) objects I approve of, (ii) objects disapprove of, and (iii) objects about which I care neither one way nor the other. It is also true that to assert of any given object X that it belongs to one group rather than another *is* to make a statement about that object. But though it is plausible to argue that this situation does constitute an exception, its appearance of doing so is a trick of language. For it is not my classification of the object X that leads me to approve of it, but rather my approval of X that leads me to classify it in the way that I do. These particular statements, these particular classifications are set up on the basis of previously established value judgments. This is a case not so much of an 'is' implying an 'ought' as of an 'ought' implying an 'is'.

If this postscript seems too technical and cryptic, there is no need to worry. The questions it raises are very specialised questions, and they have received (successfully, I hope) very specialised answers.

This chapter, like the last, has been given to discussing objections against my central thesis. As objections I have tried to answer them as best I could. But my success or failure

166

in so doing is far from being the only interest or importance of the topics discussed. The intricacy of the different ways, both evaluative and descriptive, in which the word 'moral' can be used: the various considerations and difficulties that have to be taken into account when trying to settle on a firm and consistent usage for such a key term as 'value judgment'; the way in which men of different outlooks may produce accounts of the same set of facts which, though in one sense rivals, may yet in another be impartial and imply neither approval nor disapproval—all these are topics to which one could well give several chapters each. Even the postscript raises a subject which has considerable interest from a technical point of view. All in all this chapter has produced more than its share of problems calling for further reflection.

12

REASONS, CAUSES AND FREE WILL

IF I were to try now to gather up for systematic discussion all the loose ends which I have managed to leave throughout the eleven chapters of this book, I would need at the least eleven chapters more. In the course of which, no doubt, a whole series of further questions would be raised calling for yet another eleven chapters. To this process there is in philosophy no end. There must, however, be an end to this book. So in this final chapter (before we come to the last summing up) I shall do no more than mention three of the threads which one could and should follow up; and of these there is only one which I shall pursue to any distance at all.

There is, as a first instance, the loose end of 'sincerity'. This is a notion which we used a good deal in Chapter 7 in discussing the question whether it is possible to be sincerely mistaken over a matter of values. At that time we took it for granted that the word 'sincere' would be readily understandable. But if and when we come to ask exactly what it means, we may be surprised first by the variety of answers that may be attempted and subsequently by the difficulty of providing any one answer that will be both satisfactory and clear[1]. As a matter of fact, 'sincere' raises many of the same sort of problems that are raised by the word 'moral'. It has both descriptive and evaluative functions, closely intertwined, and frequently not recognised for what they are by either party to a conversation. At the same time it is associated with the problem that we came across in Chapter 9 of how to know whether a man's expressions of feeling are

[1] Or perhaps we shall not be surprised after our experience with the very similar question with which we set out, about the meaning of 'good'.

168

genuine or merely pretence. Here, it is interesting to note, the importance that is set by some people on acts as a test of character may lead them to say that someone who does not try to do what he has previously said that he thought that he ought to do, cannot *by definition* be sincere; for them a genuine belief is one that, if the relevant situation arises, finds expression in action, any other being at best but a form of self-deceit. To other people, however, sincerity is more a matter of inner intention and attitude; and for them the question of whether such a man is sincere will be posed without necessarily being answered. But how, it may be asked, can such a question be answered if not by reference to what he may do? There are, of course, a great variety of ways by which, in different contexts, a man's sincerity may be assessed. It would, no doubt, from one point of view be simpler to treat these various criteria of evidence as in the last resort criteria of the very meaning of the word 'sincerity', that is to say as constituting the only possible conditions of its proper and meaningful application. But once again, to locate sincerity either in observable behaviour or in the inward attitudes alone would be bound to lead to serious difficulties or distortions or both. On top of all this there is the further complicating factor that one's understanding of sincerity is inevitably bound up with one's understanding of personality itself. How split can a split mind be?—and I do not mean the question in any medical sense. Can one sincerely both want to do something and at the same time be revolted by the prospect of doing it? To some it seems obvious that this is possible; to others equally obvious that in such a case, where one could be fully committed neither to doing nor to abstaining from whatever it was, neither one's intentions nor one's revulsions could be altogether sincere. The first lot of people may think of human personality as made up in most cases of separate and potentially conflicting forces; the second group may think rather in terms of some unitary core of personality which, beneath the surface conflicts, constitutes the 'real' person. But I have by now said more than enough to

169

M

indicate how extensively this particular problem may branch out.

The second point, or series of points, which clearly needs much further consideration, is concerned with the nature of principles, standards, points of view, outlooks, attitudes and purposes. All of these terms have appeared very frequently in the course of our discussions, and the first two in particular have played almost if not quite as essential a role in the argument as the term 'value judgment' itself. We have already seen, in the last chapter, the sort of trouble that may arise from allowing oneself to slip into the use of key terms without any attempt at a formal definition. It is too easy to give an appearance of tidiness and consistency to a complicated argument by making it hinge on the use of two or three key terms without noticing that one is using them first in one way and then perhaps in another. This is especially liable to happen with terms that have familiar uses in ordinary language. The more generally familiar the term, the less effort one tends to make to see just what it is doing in any particular context and the easier not to notice that it is doing something slightly different from usual. I do not in fact know of any really disastrous inconsistency to which my unsystematic use of these terms may have given rise. But without going in for a detailed investigation of all the different ways in which they may be used, I obviously cannot be sure. At any rate this too is a topic that needs looking into at much greater length, after doing which it would be more than worthwhile to come back and see to what extent the rest of our arguments would need reformulation.

Finally, there is a whole series of problems connected with the notion of 'reason'. This is another of the terms that have played a central role in our discussion of value judgments; and once again I have been content to use it on the assumption that it would be readily enough understood. But it can, of course, give rise to a very great deal of puzzled and puzzling discussion. Indeed, not a few of the many traditional problems of moral philosophy upon which we have scarcely touched, or not touched at all, turn on how we may decide to interpret this notion. And chief among these problems is that of free will. I had, in fact, originally hoped, as I explained in the very first chapter, to examine this particular problem in a second half of this book; but as it has now turned out, to do so would mean going on to an intolerable length. It would, however, be wrong to finish without trying to show at any rate something of the sort of issues that may be involved in discussing free will. So, in the confined space of the rest of this chapter only, that is what I shall try and do.

Value judgments, we have said, are essentially connected with the possibility of providing or asking for reasons—reasons based on the nature of whatever the judgments are about; and this we have taken to be one of the chief differences between value judgments and simple expressions of liking. I may be able to give a reason for liking one thing rather than another, but then again I may not; and my liking need be no less a liking for that. If, however, I wish to maintain a value judgment, I must in the last resort be prepared to back it with reasons; if I have none, I shall have either to withdraw or at least to reduce it to a straightforward expression of my own reaction of liking. A liking *may* be rational, but a value judgment *must* be.

The fact that I may be unable rationally to justify some of my likes and dislikes does not, however, necessarily mean that they must be regarded as inexplicable. To justify a viewpoint is not after all the only way of explaining it. For irrespective of whether I regard your beliefs and attitudes as reasonable or unreasonable, I may think that I know the causes in which they originate. It is true, of course, that from a colloquial point of view there are innumerable contexts in which it hardly seems to matter whether one talks of causes or reasons. But this does not mean that it is not usually possible to mark out a broad distinction between them. Why, for instance, do trees shed their leaves in autumn? Nowadays, when few people think any longer of a tree as an embodiment of some person or spirit, it would seem silly to ask the tree or the leaves for their reasons. The behaviour of trees is neither rational nor irrational; it is simply a fact, (for which an explanation can be given). In the same way, we may discover the *causes* of an avalanche without having to believe that it had a *reason* for falling; and here again, although the two words may colloquially be almost interchangeable, nearly everybody will in fact see the point of the distinction when their attention is drawn to it in this way. What happens to trees in autumn, what happens in the mountains in spring—these are facts to be recorded and, if possible, explained, but which there is little sense in trying to justify[1]. And though from one point of view I may indeed try and justify my attitudes, approvals and likings, they may also be treated from this other point of view in the same way as the falling of avalanches and the shedding of leaves; that is to say as facts that call for an explanation.

It is one thing, however, to note that there is generally a broad distinction of some sort to be drawn between reasons and causes, and very much another to work out exactly what sort of distinction it is. Some people, indeed, take the view that we can do no better than to pile up a great list of examples of the avalanche or leaf-shedding sort in which the distinction is illustrated rather than explained. But to most people this will probably seem to be at the best a second line of defence to fall back on if there really is nothing more explicit to be said—or more exactly, if all the many things that can be and have been said turn out to be themselves hopelessly unsatisfactory. For there is no real shortage of suggestions of how to tackle the problem; the trouble starts when one gets down to sorting them out.

Perhaps the suggestion that seems at first sight at least to be the simplest and most natural is that while causes are

[1] It *might* make sense to try and justify them as actions under the direct control of God—this would depend on religious or theological beliefs which are not in question here. But the *reasons* would be God's, who caused the events to take place, and not of the natural phenomena themselves.

what *make* other things happen, everyone is free to act according to their reasons or not. If, for example, I am forced to leave the room by someone picking me up and carrying me bodily outside, there is less than no point in asking me what were my reasons for leaving, unless perhaps as a deliberately unsympathetic joke. There is, moreover, a sense in which causes may seem to take precedence over reasons. I may in fact have had sufficient reasons anyhow for leaving of my own free will. But if I am forced to go by factors beyond my control, my exit is fully accounted for and any reasons that I may or may not have had become from that point of view superfluous. Only a free agent can relevantly have reasons for thinking or acting as he does. If what he does or what he thinks can be satisfactorily explained as the outcome of a certain set of causes, then he is neither free nor, strictly speaking, an agent—(if, that is to say, an agent is to be thought of as an initiator of action). Thus the difference between causes and reasons is bound up with the question of freedom. Or so, at any rate, many people have thought.

If this account is the right one, then, reasons and causes must in one sense at least be mutually exclusive of each other. If causes make things happen, then behaviour or attitudes that can be fully explained by reference to causes, cannot be counted as free; and behaviour that is not free can no more be thought of as rational than can the behaviour of trees or avalanches. Conversely, to accept somebody's position as rational is to treat him as having a certain freedom of his own, a certain independence of causes. Suppose, for instance, that your aunt keeps twenty-four cats. You may explain her collection either by referring to the emotional background that has caused her to act like this or by citing the reasons that she herself gives. But it is not possible to give *full* weight to both sorts of explanation at once. And if indeed it is the casual explanation that you take more seriously, you will most probably refer to her reasons as mere rationalisations. For if causes bring about their effects—if they really do this, then caused behaviour surely cannot be considered as free.

If this conclusion is accepted, it will of course have important moral implications. For it is generally taken for granted that moral standards apply only to people in so far as they do what they do freely and of their own accord; that no-one, for instance, can be held morally responsible for an action that he was unable to help or for not performing some action that he was not in fact free to do. On this basis it is clear that anyone who agrees that to find the causes of a man's behaviour is to show that it could not have been free, is going to run into difficulties if he wants nevertheless to make moral judgments about it. This is, indeed, precisely the difficulty with which many people feel themselves faced by recent advances in the study of the pyschological and physical bases of human character and behaviour. Can we blame a criminal if we think that we know what has caused him to be one? Moreover, not only are we now able to account for much behaviour that seemed not so long ago to be beyond normal scientific explanation, but there is at the same time every reason to suppose that we shall be able as time goes on to explain more and more and more. Comparatively few people, I imagine, worry seriously about these possibilities on the basis of the highly theoretical supposition that *all* human behaviour is ultimately causally explicable[1]. But though such wholesale determinism may not (for most of us at any rate) be an urgent practical issue, anyone may find himself confronted with some more limited instance of the problem in such a practical matter as, for example, an assessment of responsibility in a court of law. Here it is notorious that there are almost regular conflicts between those who regard crime as a symptom of some social disorder calling for remedial treatment, and those who believe on the contrary that such ideas are dangerous

---

[1] 'Theoretical' in that it is a matter of theory rather than practice. I do not intend to suggest that the theory is an unlikely one; for whether it is or not is a quite separate question.

nonsense and who stick to 'the older view that wickedness is wicked and should be punished'.

At this point, however, it might quite well be objected that I have taken it too easily for granted that the ordinary view of causes can always be adequately represented as being that they are what make other things happen. And it has to be admitted that there is something in this objection.

Consider, to take an illustration, the case of a man who leaves his wife in order to go off with his secretary. It would, as we have already noted, generally be agreed that whether he should be blamed for doing so is a question that only arises on the assumption that he was a free agent. But does this mean that he can only be blamed, or for that matter praised, for this sort of behaviour if it appears to have been without cause? Surely not, the objection might run. We might, for example, conclude that it was his wife's persistent nagging that caused him to go off, without therefore supposing that he could not have helped himself, or that his own decision played no part in the matter. Indeed, we could perfectly well say that it was his wife's nagging that brought about his decision. We could even, when one comes to think of it, speak of the causes of his action as being whatever it was that made him or drove him to do it, and still not think of him as the helpless spectator of his own elopement. And none of these ways of talking or thinking about causes are forced or extraordinary.

One way of tackling this objection might go something like this. Alright, we might say, we will agree that a man might leave his wife in the circumstances suggested. But now let us suppose that there is another man in a very similar situation. He too has a nagging wife and a (anyhow as yet) non-nagging secretary. But—he does not leave his wife. Why not? How are we to set about explaining this difference in the behaviour of the two men? We might, of course, simply say that in similar circumstances they took different decisions. But this would take us very little further on, for it can at once be asked why it was that they made up their minds differently. Because their characters were different? To say this often means little more than that they were men who normally tended to do different sorts of things and to react in different ways—men with different 'dispositions', in fact. But can we not look for causes to explain why they are the different sorts of men that they are? In some contexts and for some people the reference to character may in fact be intended as a reference to this sort of cause; character thought of perhaps as the set of basic instincts, urges and reactions that a man may inherit from his parents along with his chromosomes and genes, and which help to make him the sort of man that he is. Others would add that environmental factors, particularly early on in life, play an important part in the making of character. But can a man himself play any part in this, his own character formation? Here we are back at the question of whether we can find causes to explain the particular part that he may play. And at some such point as this we shall eventually have either to say that there is no *complete* explanation to be given, that a man by his own actions and decisions may introduce some creative element that is not wholly to be accounted for in terms of antecedent causes; or, on the other hand, to make no further bones about looking for all the remoter causes of a man's character and actions in factors finally independent of the man himself.

What exactly does this sort of answer try to do? It does not set out directly to refute any of the objector's contentions, very wisely, indeed, since within their limits they are hardly refutable. There is no point in trying to deny that we can speak of 'causing decisions', for we both can and do. It proceeds rather by drawing gradual attention to the aim of a 'complete explanation' of a man's behaviour; and by trying to show not that a free decision must be thought of as wholly inexplicable, which would be absurd, but much more plausibly that if one really thinks of it as free, one cannot at the same time regard it as *wholly* accountable for in terms of antecedent causes. It may then not unreasonably be suggested that the force of the objection arises from the fact that much behaviour may be thought of as both partially caused and partially free; and that though it might be less colloquial, it would be more accurate to talk of 'partially causing a decision'. In this way ordinary ideas about causes may after all be seen to be consistent with each other. Causes are indeed what make other things happen, but that is no reason why a (partially) free action should not be (partially) caused. It is only if something is wholly caused or determined by factors other than itself that it must be wholly unfree.

To distinguish in this way between total and partial causes is no doubt a natural enough way of talking and may, indeed, be satisfactory up to a point. But it does raise in its turn a number of further difficulties. There are, for instance, the very practical problems of whether and how an only partial responsibility should be calculated to correspond to an only partial freedom, of when and to what degree circumstances may be extenuating. But there is also a more fundamental theoretical problem, that of exactly what sense to attach to this notion of 'partial causes' if they are to be somehow interpreted as 'what partially make other things happen'. For we may be strongly tempted to suppose that if a total cause is what brings about a total effect, then each partial cause operating on its own must necessarily bring about its own partial effect, a little bit of what is or might be the total if all the other parts were there too. But very often the situation is not like this at all; and to think of it as if it were may lead to all sorts of curious confusions.

The best way of showing how and why this may be so is probably to make use of another well-known distinction, namely between necessary and sufficient conditions. There are, needless to say, a number of different ways in which these two terms may be defined. But roughly speaking a sufficient condition of an event is one whose presence is on its own enough to show that the event in question either has taken place, is taking place now or will take place in the future. A necessary condition on the contrary is one whose *absence* shows that the event either can't take or can't have taken place[1]. People sometimes tend to use these terms in a narrower way than this, thinking of a sufficient condition as one that is sufficient actually to bring an event about, and of a necessary condition as one that is needed to do so; and so very naturally suppose that they must always precede in time the events of which they are conditions, or at least be simultaneous with them. But it is on the whole better not to impose this restriction, not least because without it the two terms turn out to be neatly correlative to each other independently of their temporal relations. It is, for example, a *necessary* condition of my watch keeping time all day that it should have been wound up this morning; if it had not been wound up, it would not be going now. So conversely the fact that it is going now is *sufficient* to show that it must have been wound up. Or to take another example to show this relationship working in the opposite direction in time, a night of steady rain is sufficient to leave the grass wet in the morning; so, working backwards to what the weather must have been like, the grass would have to be wet in the morning for it to have rained. This is the pattern of argument that a detective may use to break somebody's alibi by showing that something is not in the condition in which it would necessarily have been if his story had been true.

(The second of these two examples raises a further point which, though not perhaps of immediate and urgent relevance, is an important one and should be noted. A night's rain will certainly leave the grass wet in the morning, but it is not the only thing that could do so. A heavy dew, for

[1] It is, as we know, tiresome and even dangerous to use the same term in more than one way in the same general context. However, it has to be noted that the word 'necessary' *is* frequently used in this sense, (to mean something like 'prerequisite'), as well as in the quite different sense in which analytic propositions are said to be logically necessary. (See Chapter 3.)

178

instance, or my watering the lawn with a hose could also have this result. In other words there may be more than one possible sufficient condition for one and the same event, and, what is more, there may sometimes be several of them present together. (It may start to rain just as I am putting away my hose.) It follows from this, and from the nature of the link between sufficient and necessary conditions, that it may not be the presence of one unique set of conditions that is necessary for the occurrence of some event, but only the presence of one of several alternatives. I don't have to have a *pen* to be able to write this sentence. A typewriter would do, or a pencil, or . . . and there are, of course, a number of other possibilities. But it *is* necessary that at least one of these alternatives should be available.)

To return, however, to the more immediate point. How far does this distinction between necessary and sufficient conditions correspond to that between partial and total causes? In many ways the correspondence is reasonably close. In particular there is a sense in which the sufficient condition of an event may be said to be the sum total of all the necessary conditions[1]. This is simply because no condition can be sufficient if anything really necessary is lacking; while if, contrariwise, every condition that is necessary is without exception present, they must together be sufficient. On the other hand, while it may be natural to suppose that a partial cause must bring about a corresponding partial effect there is no special reason to suppose that the presence of single necessary conditions should on their own lead to anything further at all. A sufficient condition resembles a total cause to the extent that its presence is a sufficient indication of the existence of something else; but a necessary condition provides only the possibility of the existence of something else, a possibility that may quite well remain unfulfilled. I must have a pen or a pencil or something of the sort if I am to get this chapter written; but my mere posses-

[1] This would have to be stated in a more complicated way if we wished to take proper account of the preceding paragraph.

sion of a pen may lead only to some inartistic doodling or even to nothing at all.

This points to an important aspect of those explanations that consist in a reference to some necessary condition only. They are given typically in answer to questions of the form "How was so-and-so possible, how could it have happened like that?". "How on earth", for example, "was he able to write all that ?"—"It is because he bought himself a new pen yesterday afternoon". The question to which this explanation is an answer asked not what brought it about that I wrote five incoherent pages, but simply how it was possible; in the context, presumably, of what had been believed to be my lack of writing material. In one sense certainly this explanation may fairly be described as causal. On the other hand, the event to which the explanation refers in no way limits my freedom of action; on the contrary, it extends it. In a way, of course, this is obvious enough. But it is something over which we may easily become puzzled if, using the notion of 'partial cause' rather than that of 'necessary condition', we try somehow to square this use of 'cause' with its well-established connections with the ideas of 'making happen' and 'bringing about'.

The fact that references to causes are often in effect references to necessary rather than to sufficient conditions, does a good deal to explain how causal explanations of this sort may seem to imply little or no limitation of the freedom of the agent concerned. But what now about 'complete explanations' or explanations in terms of sufficient conditions? The situation here is by no means straightforward. There are a variety of theoretical difficulties which may be involved; but the main problem lies in the fact that the notion of 'complete explanation' is one which is bound in practice to vary depending on what and how much is taken for granted in the relevant context. Why is the lawn wet? Normally it will be sufficient to reply that I have just turned the hose on it, and superfluous to mention that the hose was properly fixed to the tap, that the tap was running and so on, necessary though these conditions certainly are. If, however, yesterday you yourself had turned the water off at the main, you may *not* find sufficient the explanation that I had turned on the hose. Indeed, you may already know this and I may know that you know, and neither of us therefore regard it now as worth explicit mention. In which case I may be able to explain that it was turning the tap at the main that caused the lawn to be flooded; though obviously, unless it is tacitly assumed as well that the hose had been turned on the lawn, the tap-turning at the main could not on its own be said to have caused any such thing. This is a good illustration of the way in which all explanation of specific states of affairs takes place against a background of tacit assumption; and how what in one context may appear as a sufficient condition in itself may in another be no more than one of the necessary items to be included in any more complete or sufficient explanation. Similarly with prediction. If you press the switch the light will go on; in normal circumstances we may become so unreflectingly confident of the success of this prediction as to find it a little strange to think of it as a prediction at all. But in a period of frequent and irregular load-shedding, for instance, we may no longer be so certain; and it may become very much to the point if we are able to support our prediction with information about what is going on at the power station, information which in theory is always of equal relevance, but which in practice may often be redundant.

Precisely the same considerations, of course, relate to the notion of 'total cause'. What on one set of assumptions may be presented as the total cause, the complete explanation, of an event, may appear as an only partial cause on another. Compare, for example, these three assertions: (i) "Her nagging was a contributory cause of the break-up of their marriage"; (ii) "Her nagging caused him to leave her"; (iii) "Her nagging was the cause of his leaving her". In the first sentence, while the use of the word 'cause' implies clearly enough that the marriage did in fact break up, the wife's nagging is referred to as only one of the (alternatively) necessary conditions. In the second sentence, the focus of attention is narrowed down; maybe there were other causes of at least equal importance, the thing is that we are not talking about them now. In the third sentence, the nagging is explicitly taken as a decisive, a sufficient condition. But all three sentences could quite fairly be used by different people to refer to one and the same event. For even in the third instance there must obviously be an endless number of other conditions that might have been mentioned, even though beside the wife's nagging they may seem to some onlookers to be unimportant, trite, irrelevant—just part of the understood background against which the break-up is to be explained. This line, however, between the background situation and the event to be explained can have no hard and fast existence in the facts themselves; and just where it is drawn in each context is bound to depend on our interests, assumptions and information in the context in question.

All this helps to explain how it is that while causal language does provide a temptation to argue that caused behaviour cannot be free, it can at the same time be used in a way that seems quite compatible with freely willed decisions. In the first place the distinction may be drawn between total and partial causes, enabling us to talk of behaviour that is free within limits. Secondly, however, this ideal of a 'partial cause' can sometimes be very confusing, and it may often be clearer to talk rather of necessary conditions. For there is no reason why a necessary condition should as such and on its own have any positive tendency to bring about anything else at all. Still, it is a natural use of language to refer to any important influencing or even permissive condition as a causal factor; and so we may slip easily into the apparently puzzling position of talking of causes which may not exactly bring about their effects. Finally, what is counted as a sufficient condition, or total cause, and what as a necessary condition, or partial cause, must depend in each particular context on a balance of relevance and assumption. And this means, among other things, that anyone who in a given case is convinced of the crucial relevance of a free decision, may hope to tip the balance in the direction of partial causation without having to dismiss the explanations offered as completely invalid.

Whatever else may have been shown by this discussion, it seems clear that even the 'ordinary' view of causation is on closer inspection by no means simple or straightforward. In particular, we have seen something of the difficulties there may be in knowing just how to apply a notion such as that of a complete explanation. Nevertheless, we have in spite of this in the end left more or less intact the view that in so far as behaviour *can* be completely accounted for in causal terms, then at any rate it cannot be free. Even this view, however, has been and still is very much disputed. It is disputed most seriously on the basis of a certain sort of analysis of what is involved in any judgment that one event is the cause or effect of another. This analysis has in fact a great many complicated ramifications. But since it is so often used to support an undeniably powerful claim—a wholly different sort of claim from the one we have just considered—that there is never any incompatibility between reasons and causes as such, between determinism and free will, I must at least try to explain in as short a space as I can what sort of analysis it is. This will not, I fear, be easy; but not, I hope, impossibly difficult either, since the interpretation in question is a typically empiricist one and thus very much in line with the account of analytic and synthetic propositions with which we are already familiar.

Let us assume, then, that to discover that one event is causally related to another is to discover a fact about the world. (This is not a very startling assumption, but it had better be made explicit.) It may now very naturally be pointed out that the only way in which such facts may be discovered or substantiated is, as we have already noted indeed, on the basis of the appropriate observations. What sorts of observations would be necessary or relevant? It is generally agreed that the most important one of all must be that the one event is *regularly* followed or preceded by the other, that whenever the cause occurs so too does the effect. We should, for instance, have little reason to say on a particular occasion that Mr. Smith's death had been caused by prussic acid, if in other cases of a similar type the taking of prussic acid was not followed by death as a regular matter of course. Naturally, the observations necessary to ensure both that the given instance is of the type supposed and that the sequence is truly regular, may involve quite elaborate systems of tests. But—and this is the crucial step in the argument—such tests, however complicated, can only be directed to the most rigorous possible confirmation of the central fact that A is indeed regularly followed by B. For only if we are confident in the regularity of a sequence do we talk of it as causal or of the generalisation in which it is formulated as a causal generalisation. Once, however, we are satisfied that these observations have been accurately made, what else, it is asked, can we possibly hope to observe? Even in the classic case of one billiard ball hitting another, all that can really be seen is one event (their impact) followed by a second (their departure on their respective paths). All this means that in the last resort causal generalisations must be based simply on repeated observations and a belief that future observations will give similar results. As to the observations that have already been made, they might in theory have been different, and if they had been, our causal laws would naturally have been different too. In the same way it is always logically possible that future observations may turn out to be different from what our presently accepted laws would lead us to predict, in which case our laws will have to be rethought and formulated afresh.[1] It is in this very way that fundamental scientific advances may be made. So it would be very misleading to talk of causal

[1] Compare our earlier discussions of why it is always logically possible that the contrary of what is asserted in any synthetic proposition should be or should have been the case.

laws as forcing events into any particular pattern. If we must talk about 'forcing' at all, it might be more accurate to talk of phenomena, (that is appearances, or the observations that have been made), forcing us to frame the causal laws that we do.

So on this analysis the situation is that causal generalisations can only be justified on the basis of the observation of regular sequences; and that only on the basis of such generalisations may we in turn either explain or predict the occurrences of particular events in particular instances. It is worth emphasising, incidentally, that it is an essential feature of this interpretation that explanation and prediction should go together in this way. "It was the taking of prussic acid that caused his death"—"If he takes prussic acid, he will certainly die". Explanations are concerned with present or past events, predictions have to do with the future. But in either case the so-called logical pattern is the same; a particular case is shown to be an instance of some general rule. Usually when we talk of causes, explanations or predictions, the generalisations on which they may be based receive no explicit mention. But their role is fundamental. If A is always followed by B, if the taking of large doses of prussic acid is always followed by death, then to explain Mr. Smith's death in this way is to show how it could have been predicted if we had had the information in advance; conversely, to predict his death on this basis is to show how, when he has swallowed his acid, it can then be explained. If A was only sometimes followed by B, then all we could do would be to provide a possible partial explanation or a hesitant provisional prediction— unless, of course, we had a reliable theory taking into account a wide variety of factors and providing other general rules for when to expect exceptions.

We should now be ready for the final stage in this argument; namely that when once we have realised that causal generalisations, of which all particular causal explanations or predictions are but the applications in individual cases,

185

are themselves based simply on the observation of regular sequences, we may see that it is after all possible to think of caused behaviour as free. For when seen in this light the two terms turn out not to conflict with each other. The opposite of caused behaviour would be behaviour that fitted into no sort of regular pattern, random behaviour about which no generalisation could be made. But it is only in a very peculiar sense that random behaviour might be called free, and it would be even more peculiar to think of it as essentially rational or responsible. There is, on the other hand, nothing odd about the idea of a man freely following an entirely regular way of life, so that all who know him could predict his behaviour from one day to another with the utmost confidence. As it is often put "the opposite of cause is chance, while the opposite of freedom is constraint; and to identify the two is nothing but a confusion".

This version of the 'regularity interpretation' of causality is obviously enough a sharply oversimplified affair. It would, to take one instance, be very misleading to suggest that our knowledge of what happens when one billiard ball hits another, was based solely and directly on a long experience of billiards. Indeed, simple isolated generalisations that do rest on nothing but a series of observations all of exactly the same sort as each other, have little explanatory power and often may not even be very reliable. (A sad story is told of a turkey who had noted that when the farmer came in the morning it was always a sign of food, and the surprise that it got at Christmas when this most regular of sequences was broken.) In fact, once we know what sort of things billiard balls are, there is a wide variety of experience of the behaviour of moving bodies that may help us to account for or to predict their movements on the billiard table. And if we wish to work out more exactly what they are likely to do after impact, there is available a great deal of intricate and very general theory founded on the laws of motion, whose power and reliability arises precisely from the fact that it can be applied to and confirmed in an infinite number and variety of different situations. The relations between a particular instance, the generalisation or generalisations of which it is an instance and the supporting body of theory may become very complicated, and involve more often than not some highly sophisticated mathematics. But in spite of all this it can still be argued that we are bound in the end to find ourselves back at the observation of regular sequences; if not perhaps of the behaviour of such specialised objects as billiard balls, then more generally of that of any kind of body with certain specified properties. It is, of course, true that if an object of a certain size, shape and weight strikes another object with equally definite specifications at a certain angle, with a certain velocity and within certain definite conditions, then strictly as a matter of theory the outcome of the collision is completely determined. But such determinism or 'forcing' as there may be belongs only to our own theoretical construction. *If* our theory is correct, (as within its area of application nobody may doubt it to be), and if it is applicable to the particular objects in question, then it does follow—logically or analytically, in fact—that they must behave in a certain definite way; for if they did not, then *ipso facto* the theory would be shown to be incorrect or at any rate inapplicable. But they cannot be forced either by each other or by us or by the theory itself to support and verify it in this way. We may continue to observe that the sequences they follow conform as before to the pattern of generalisations created to describe their behaviour. But this, in the end, is all.

Happily, however, we do not for our present purposes need to go into all the complicated arguments and counter-arguments for and against this interpretation of causality. For I am not here trying to argue either that there is or that there is not any incompatibility between free will and causation; but merely to explain some of the basic reasons why so many empiricist philosophers have maintained that the truth of determinism, (that is, of the assertion that every event has a cause), need imply no restriction on the making of free and responsible choices. And all elaboration aside, the central thesis of this doctrine may be put briefly enough—that neither causes, explanations nor predictions need as such compel.

"Causes do not compel". If this analysis is right, then is there nothing whatsoever in what I have taken to be the ordinary view that causes are 'what make other things happen'? It has at any rate to be admitted that it does feel oddly uncomfortable to insist in reverse that causes do not make anything happen; for it is undeniable that the words 'cause' and 'make' are very closely linked by the customary rules of meaning of our ordinary language. Some people may feel that this in itself constitutes a powerful objection to the causes-do-not-compel sort of theory. All the same, we must not overlook the possibility that a supporter of this theory who is nevertheless determined to preserve these linkings of normal speech, may in fact analyse 'make happen' in very much the same way as he analyses 'cause'. An assertion, for example, such as "Those kippers made me feel sick" might roughly be construed as "Whenever I eat more than one kipper, I subsequently feel sick; I ate two kippers this morning and did feel sick afterwards". This leaves us as before with nothing more than particular instances of observed sequences, the only special point to note being that the observations here include observations of the observer's own feelings. One may even go on to claim that it is possible to produce a similar analysis for all other concepts in which that of 'cause' is in any way involved, such, for instance, as any transitive verb. And though this would, of course, be a pretty tall order, the claim should not be too lightly dismissed; for even those who feel most convinced that it is outrageous, may yet find it very hard to show exactly where it goes wrong.

For myself, I may as well confess that I am not altogether happy about analysing determinism and free will into apparently harmonious compatibility. But neither am I altogether happy about rejecting this analysis. One day, I hope, I may be able to come to some rather clearer and more definite conclusion about this than I have been able to reach up to date. Meanwhile, though it may seem to you to be preposterous to argue that not even total or sufficient causes really make anything happen, or that if they do, it is only because 'to make' is not 'to constrain', you should still remember that the empiricist analysis is not performed in the spirit of some intellectual conjuring trick. It is on the contrary a serious attempt to give systematic weight to two inescapably important considerations: (i) That there is in the last resort no way of controlling the truth or falsity of any assertion about the world other than through observations, and (ii) That the very meaning of any assertion whatsoever must somehow be linked to and limited by the ways in which it may be either confirmed or disproved.

This at any rate is as far as we can take the discussion in this book. So let me now simply restate what I have been trying to do in this chapter. I started, then, by pointing out—quite superfluously, no doubt—that in philosophy, especially in a not very long introductory discussion, there are bound to appear an increasing number of loose ends. Of these I mentioned three as calling very obviously for further discussion; sincerity, the nature of principles, purposes and standards, and the relations between the notions of 'reason' and 'cause'. This last question is the only one that I have considered at any length, and I did so because of the way in which it is in its turn entangled with problems about free will, problems which are of central importance to any moral philosophy. To discuss them at all systematically would, of course, need a much larger book. So what I have tried to do has been simply to explain something of the nature of the framework within which such a discussion must take place. For these purposes I started from an interpretation of the ordinary view of causes as being that they are 'what make other things happen', and from the assumption that only a free agent can be thought of as acting on the basis of reasons. On these assumptions there seems clearly to be some sort of incompatibility between reasons and causes, arising out of their different relations with free will; and any such incompatibility would seem to have very serious implications for judgments of moral responsibility. But—is this in fact the right way in which to pose the problem? For both assumptions may be called into question. Much more, for instance, would need to be said about whether 'reason' really is so intimately connected with 'freedom' as I have made out, and, if so, the exact nature of the connection. But it is on the whole the nature of causal explanation that has given rise to the more striking confusions and controversy. So I have in fact spent most of my time in talking about the idea of 'cause'; in particular, about two of the various arguments that have been put forward to suggest that causation and free will may after all get along together perfectly well. The first of these was the common sense sort of argument that much behaviour may be only partially caused; which is within its limits a very reasonable line to take. Unfortunately, though, the notion of 'partial explanation' is one that may only too easily get out of common sensible control, and I have tried to illustrate some of the less immediately visible snags that can sometimes crop up by introducing the alternative notions of necessary and sufficient conditions. Secondly, there was the much more radical sort of argument, based on an empiricist analysis of causal judgments, that there is really no sense in supposing that causes, partial, total or whatever, have any tendency to compel. For, it is said, any causal explanation or prediction must in the end be based on the observation of one thing regularly following upon another in sequences whose continued regularity can never be unconditionally guaranteed.

But I shall not attempt to go through these arguments again, even in summary form. There are instead just two points that I should add. First, one that I have already made in passing, but which needs to be re-emphasised, namely, that there are many contexts in which the terms 'cause' and 'reason' are for all colloquial purposes interchangeable, and many others in which, though there may seem to be a distinction, it is extraordinarily hard actually to make. Typical examples of such contexts are those in which questions are asked or explanations given in terms of motives. Are motives to be understood as reasons for or causes of motivated actions? In a casual everyday way one tends, I think, to regard them now as one, now as the other, without anyhow knowing exactly just what difference it would make which one thought of them as. It is not surprising that different philosophers have given different answers to this very question. (It is also worth noting that there is an important sense in which causal judgments are themselves inherently rational. "Like cause, like effect" expresses one of the rules governing the meaning of the term 'cause', and makes it impossible to talk of two situations identical in every respect except only that in one case A causes B while in the other it does not.) Secondly and finally, I should once more repeat that the problems I have here mentioned are only a few of the many that may arise in connection with free will. Does it really follow from the very meaning of the term 'moral' that moral judgments can only be made of freely responsible agents? *Could* one be held responsible for a completely uncaused action? What sort of connections are there between responsibility, praise, blame and, in particular, punishment? And so on and so on. All things considered it is just as well that this book must have an end.

13

RETROSPECT

IT now only remains to take a last look back over the
argument as a whole, to restate it in its broadest outlines
and ... to apologise for all the obscurities that, I fear, I must
have left behind.

The problem around which the whole discussion has
revolved has, of course, been that of the nature of value
judgments. This, however, was far too general a problem to
start by tackling head on, and so we set out from the more
specific and hence more manageable question of the meaning
of 'good'. Questions of this sort, we explained in Chapter 2,
questions that is to say about meaning, are better understood
as questions about the uses of words rather than as about
the nature of things. This is an important distinction,
because words can obviously enough be used in a number of
different ways and very often their primary function is not to
record, name or describe the nature of things at all. But it is
virtually impossible in such cases to see clearly what their
function is, if we fail to distinguish between matters relating
to language and matters relating to (non-linguistic) fact.

Even after these preliminaries we still did not embark
directly on the question of the meaning of 'good'. Instead
Chapter 3 was for the most part spent on introducing and
explaining the generally accepted classification of statements
as either analytic or synthetic; analytic if their truth or
falsity depended solely on the meanings of the terms employed, synthetic if it depended on the result of some observation relating to the facts that they claimed to be about.
This was undeniably to take a somewhat roundabout route.
Most people would no doubt have been perfectly prepared
to accept the dictionary account of 'good' as the most

general term of commendation in the English language and to have left it at that. The trouble was, however, that many of them would have wanted at the same time to maintain that there was a firm, 'objective' sense in which assertions of the type "such and such a thing is good" could be true or false; and so it was clear that one could come to no satisfactory conclusion about the meaning of 'good' before making up one's mind whether and how such a claim might be justified. It was this aspect of the problem that led us on to the classification of statements. For statements, or propositions, may very naturally be taken to be any expressions of which it could in principle be said that they were false or true. Hence, if a value judgment can be true or false, it seems that it must be some sort of statement; and so it was relevant to enquire as to the different sorts of statement that there are.

This, then, was the theme of Chapter 3; that there were broadly speaking two very different sorts of proposition, analytic on the one hand and synthetic on the other. The obvious next step to take was to ask whether value judgments could plausibly be classified under either of these heads; and this was the question we considered in Chapter 4. I tried to provide in the course of this chapter a variety of arguments designed to show that neither of these alternatives was satisfactory. But powerful though their cumulative effect seemed (to me at any rate) to be, I could not in all honesty claim by the end of the chapter that I had actually *proved* it to be impossible to treat value judgments as statements. For in the last resort I had to admit that my arguments rested on an assumption, the assumption that there was a clear distinction between evaluation and description, that it was, as the slogan has it, impossible validly to derive an 'ought' from an 'is'. And this assumption still remained to be proved.

Nevertheless, it seemed as an assumption to be fair enough to go on with; and so we proceeded on the basis that value judgements could not sensibly be counted as statements. This left us in need of an alternative account. And so in the following Chapter 5 I made use of Mr. Hare's distinction between meaning and criteria, in accordance with which we were able to say that the *meaning* of 'good' lay in its primarily commendatory (and non-descriptive) function, but that the *criteria* were provided by those characteristics of objects or behaviour for which they were commended. Among the virtues of this account was the way in which it enabled us to explain why it makes no sense to distinguish between otherwise similar objects simply on the grounds that one of them is good while the other is not; and to see in this fact one important sense at least in which value judgments are essentially rational.

This, then, provided us with an answer to our original question; "What does it mean to say of anything that it is good?" But we were still left with one extremely important loose end, namely the question of whether it made any sense to talk of value judgments as either true or false. We had said earlier that the notions of truth and falsity were very closely tied to that of a statement; and so indeed they are. On the other hand, there would be an absurd side to any theory which simply and straightforwardly denied that there could be any sense at all in talking of the truth or falsity of value judgments; for to do so is a familiar and, in normal circumstances, intelligible feature of common speech. The only other possibility was to suggest an alternative account of the use of the word 'true'. And in Chapter 6 I did in fact put forward the (not original) suggestion that this term could best be understood as being, like 'good', a value-word, one whose meaning lay in its provision of a very special sort of guaranteed confirmation; while the criteria on which such confirmations might be based would naturally vary from context to context and, above all, according to whether it was an analytic or synthetic proposition or a value judgment that was being confirmed. There was, I argued, a great deal to be said for this interpretation of 'true'. But I had also to point out that it would be unreasonable to expect it to reflect every aspect of the normal associations of the word. For there is after all no reason whatsoever to assume that all the habitual cross-associations to be found within ordinary language should be consistent with each other. It would on the contrary be far more surprising if they were.

After all this Chapter 7 provided something of an interlude, an interlude in which we discussed the problem of whether on the basis of the account that I had just put forward it could still make sense to talk of someone being sincerely mistaken over a matter of right and wrong. The question is, of course, interesting and important for its own sake. But it had at this stage of the argument the additional interest and importance of providing a sort of testing ground on which to try out our mastery in a different context of the theory of which we had just given an outline. In Chapter 8 we were back at the main business again, now at last to tackle directly what is in my view at any rate the real heart of the problem, this question of the nature of the distinction on which everything else must rest, between evaluation and description. In this chapter we discussed the (at present) widely accepted view that the distinction is nothing else than a matter of logic. It was, I agreed, indeed a matter of logic that "nothing can appear in the conclusion of a valid deductive argument that was not already contained in the premises". But it still remained to be shown that the distinction between description and evaluation was really such that the one could not be held to contain the other; and this I concluded it was not possible to demonstrate by logic alone.

If not by logic, how then? The answer that I suggested and tried to elaborate in Chapter 9 was that there was in the end no substitute for the simple recognition that to record on the one hand and to approve or disapprove on the other were two irreducibly different ways of approaching the facts. In making this suggestion I did, however, try to explain why from some points of view it was undeniably a sort of second-best; for it was never wholly satisfactory to have no other resource but to appeal to people to examine their own experience and to "see if you do not see what I see in mine". Nevertheless, I tried at the same time to show why this seems to be a distinction that few could fail to recognise in some contexts at any rate when the issue is fairly put; and, slightly more speculatively perhaps, the way in which it should in principle be possible to bring anyone who has once recognised the distinction, subsequently to see that it must therefore be applicable to all other contexts too. I had, however, to concede in concluding Chapter 9 that there were a number of extremely important objections that could be brought against my procedures up to date. The most far reaching of them was that the term 'approval', on which I had been very heavily relying, was much too indefinite and vague to bear the weight of the argument. This objection I attempted to face in Chapter 10—with what degree of success I am still, I confess, unsure. At any rate I tried in this chapter to clarify the meaning of 'approval', comparing it in particular with the meaning of 'liking'; but also to explain why it was not altogether essential that it should receive a completely unambiguous, sharp-edged definition for my argument to work. Chapter 11 was also concerned with objections. There was one that centred round the meaning of the word 'moral'; one that arose from an underlying inconsistency in my previous uses of the key term 'value judgment', and the obscurity in which I had left the question of the nature of its association with the notion of 'approval'; and one that was based on what I would agree to be the indisputable fact that in some contexts alternative ways of recording what is believed to be the case, may be inextricably linked with different general attitudes or world-views. I did my best to suggest how one might deal with all these objections; though in the case of the second one in particular, not without a certain embarrassment.

This brought to an end the central discussion of the book. 'Brought to an end' rather than 'concluded', for there were, of course, many loose ends left over—and some important ones at that—each of which might in its turn give rise to a whole series of further chapters. One of these loose ends concerned the meaning of the term 'reason', and its relations with the notion of 'cause'; two terms which are often interchangeable, but which are also often not. This is a question which leads on to what I would take to be the other main problem of moral philosophy, that of the nature, meaning and relevance of the freedom of the will. It would very obviously have been impossible to have attempted any systematic discussion of this problem, or rather family of problems, in one concluding chapter. But it would have been wrong on the other hand for it to have received no mention at all. And so in Chapter 12 I tried to explain (*a*) something of the complexities of the ordinary notion of what might constitute a complete causal explanation, and (*b*) the basis on which so many empiricist philosophers have maintained the at first sight surprising thesis that there is not in fact any incompatibility between free will and determinism, between reason and cause.

So we arrived at Chapter 13—that of which we are now at the end, and with it the end of the book. There is, however, just one final point which it is worth repeating. This has been intended as an introduction to a certain range of problems. At the very best any solutions that I may have suggested, have been no more than solutions in outline. They leave many details to be filled in, many details to be disputed—if, indeed, it is not wished to dispute the outlines themselves. I should be glad, of course, if they turn out to be broadly acceptable. But I shall also be glad if they *are* vigorously disputed. For the purpose of this introduction has been above all to show what is the nature of the problems to which the solutions are proposed; and it will have been doubly fulfilled if anyone is stimulated into thinking a dispute worthwhile.

Appendix

FURTHER REFLECTIONS ON "THE MEANING OF 'TRUE'"

AMONG the comments made by Professor O'Connor when he read my original typescript were two which he described as 'major'. But not only are they important in themselves; they provide at the same time an excellent illustration of the sort of discussions and disagreements that arise between philosophers. So I am most grateful to him for allowing me to quote here an extract from one of his entirely informal letters, as well as the unfair luxury of the last word—at any rate within the covers of this book.

The extract in question runs as follows:—

"(i). I am not convinced by your Chapter 6 on 'Truth'. It seems to me that the analogy between 'true' as applied to factual statements and as applied to value judgments breaks down at this very important point. 'True' implies that the guarantees one offers are *publicly acceptable* and *conclusive*. But this is not usually the case with the reasons one offers to support disputed moral judgments.

"Of course, if you pursue this point, it leads to discussing what counts as a good reason in moral contexts. And this links up with

"(ii). In your penultimate chapter, you might put in a bit more on the way that reasons are causes and also on the most important criteria for distinguishing good reasons from bad or irrelevant ones."

As to this second point, I still hope as a matter of fact that ɪmay not be too unreasonable to leave it over as far as this book is concerned. This is not to say that the question raised is not of great importance; for, of course, it is. It is also a very intricate one. For suppose, to take one example, that somebody says that so-and-so is a good man because he likes collecting stamps. Should we regard this as a bad reason, a mad reason, an irrelevant reason or not a reason at all? What anyway are the differences between these four categories? Or, to take one other example, we should probably feel confident enough that "because the potatoes are burnt" is no reason for maintaining that "the steak is good"; but just how should we justify this confidence? What sort of criteria lie behind judgments of relevance? Could there possibly be any sort of general answer to this question? And so on and so on. But one must stop somewhere even if only provisionally. And all these questions, important and intriguing as they are, seem to me to be questions that one should *go on* to pursue.

The point about 'truth', however, is somewhat different. For this is not a matter of something which I might and very possibly should have discussed, but to which I have not in fact got around; but one rather of something which I have said, being challenged as misleading or even wrong. So here I do feel obliged to look again at what I said in Chapter 6.

In that chapter my main suggestion came in effect to this: "We may say that the meaning of 'true' lies in this special sort of affirmatory or confirmatory function . . . , while the criteria on which such confirmations may be based will obviously vary, as in the case of 'good', from context to context. It follows that to say that it is true that such and such a thing is good, is to do exactly what one would be doing in saying that any other assertion was true; it is to affirm the assertion in question in a way that offers a fully committed guarantee." (p.86). But—O'Connor's objection seems to be—it is not only the types of criteria that differ; so, far more importantly, do the sorts of guarantee that are available. For, as he put it in a subsequent passage, "Reasons given in support of factual statements tend, as they accumulate, to establish the fact, while reasons given in support of value judgments tend only to form a decision." I myself, of

199

course, have insisted throughout on the importance of making and maintaining some firm sort of distinction between judgments of value and statements of fact. So the point of the objection must be that my suggested analysis of 'true' would inconsistently serve to blur the very distinction which I have been trying to recommend.

But suppose that we abandon this suggested analysis; what then are the consequences? We should have the choice between (i) maintaining that the word 'true' has at least two largely, if not totally, unrelated meanings, one for use with value judgments and the other for use with synthetic and (perhaps) analytic propositions; (ii) proposing some other function than that of providing guaranteed confirmations or affirmations, which the word might fulfil equally well throughout its whole range of contexts; and (iii) insisting that value judgments can never properly be said to be true or false at all. The first of these suggestions is not really very plausible; and though I have no doubt that it would be possible to put the 'guaranteed affirmation' account very much better than I have managed to put it, I cannot at the moment think of any seriously different alternative that would not seem much further fetched. However, it looks very much as if it is in any case the third suggestion that O'Connor would favour. And though he would no doubt agree that people do in fact very often talk and think of value judgments as either true or false, he would be able to explain this as a natural corollary of the common confusion between values and facts.

Now this is not an impossible nor even an implausible line to take. For, as I myself pointed out in Chapter 6, the words 'true' and 'fact' *are* very closely tied together. Moreover, "normally, someone who says that a fact is something that is the case, thinks of it as being the case irrespective of what anybody may think or feel about it" (p. 78); and this, according to my own argument, is precisely what values are not. So I was perhaps putting it somewhat mildly when I admitted, as of course I had to, that my account of the meaning of 'true' did "fail to take into consideration certain aspects of its significance in ordinary speech", namely those aspects which are associated with the reference to "what we may call the nature of things as they are, existing in the way they do, independently of anyone's thoughts or feelings about them". (p. 91). And it is clear from this that I must have considerable sympathy with anyone who wishes to restrict the use of 'true' to contexts in which it may retain with a good conscience all, or at least nearly all, of its familiar links with 'facts'.

If, however, we did restrict the use of 'true' to our dealings with synthetic (and perhaps analytic) propositions, we should still have to give some account of its meaning or function. And the account that O'Connor would seem to suggest—namely that it used to offer a 'publicly acceptable and conclusive' form of guarantee of the factual (or analytic) assertions to which alone it may be attached runs into at least two very considerable difficulties.

(a). It often happens that somebody may stick to some improbable story with the obstinate insistence "But it *is* true all the same". It is clear that he would be offering some sort of up to the hilt guarantee. But his guarantee may very well fail to appear as either acceptable or conclusive, and in fact be rejected. Moreover, and this is the more important point, the speaker himself may have no illusion that he can produce any worth while evidence whatsoever; to do so is in the nature of some cases not only difficult but impossible. A man who has, for instance, a long criminal record, may on a particular occasion pick up a lost pocket-book with the genuine intention of returning it to its owner. But if he is perhaps arrested and questioned before he has had time to do so, nobody is likely to believe him nor he likely to expect them to. "Yet", he may say, "whether anyone believes it or not, what I have said is true." In other words, the mere fact that a man insists that a particular story is true may carry with it no implication at all of any offer of a 'publicly acceptable and conclusive guarantee'.

201

o

What is offered is the speaker's word; but this can not on its own imply the existence of any publicly acceptable grounds for the acceptance of the offer.

(b). On the other hand, there are many contexts and situations in which the confirmation offered in support of a value judgment may as a matter of actual fact be received as 'publicly acceptable and conclusive'. Of course, it remains open to anyone to maintain that such matters *ought* never to be taken as publicly settled. But this surely is a value judgment itself. For some people may well feel that there are certain principles to which reference *should* be taken as publicly acceptable and conclusive; and this not necessarily because they regard these principles as somehow embedded in facts, but simply because that is the way that they feel about their values. There is naturally no logically conclusive reason why anyone's claim to public allegiance to a value judgment of his own should actually be accepted; but neither is there any such reason why his claim should not be made. In this one respect at least the position seems to be very much the same as it is in regards to factual statements.

As against this O'Connor might, rightly, insist that there is a sense in which I could never, so to speak, rub your nose in a value in the way in which I might often be able to rub it into a fact. You do not believe me when I say that the cat is on the mat? Very well then, I shall make you come and have a look. Though it may be hard to formulate precisely, there is undeniably this sense in which we should say that matters of fact have an independence of a sort that values do not. And for this reason they may be said to constitute a sort of court of ultimate or conclusive appeal to which one should in principle be able to refer any dispute over the authenticity of a factual statement. For disputed value judgments, on the other hand, there is even in principle no such court of ultimate and independent reference.

What this amounts to, however, is a further elaboration of the position that synthetic propositions and value judgments may be confirmed in different ways and within quite different sorts of limits. No doubt, in many cases of factual dispute the guarantee given by one side or the other may be backed up by considerations that put it beyond intelligible question by anyone who speaks the same language[1]; (e.g. I take you to see the cat which I told you was on the mat). But merely to assure you that what I said about the cat was true is in itself to produce neither cat nor mat, nor to imply that I can do so. In saying that any particular account of the facts is true, one is but offering a guarantee of that account. And although naturally I cannot guarantee a value judgment *on the same basis* as I might a statement of fact, I may still affirm it as beyond question or reservation; not, of course, beyond question in the sense that it would be logically impossible in this case for anyone speaking the same language to disagree with my judgment, but in the sense that I might be prepared conclusively to condemn anyone who did disagree.

Indeed, O'Connor's comment might be reformulated to lose most of its sting: "Reasons given in support of factual statements tend, as they accumulate, to establish the fact, while reasons given in support of a value judgment tend to *establish a decision.*" Of course facts and values are different. But though it is no more possible to establish a value in the same way as one might establish a fact than it is to establish a fact in the same way as one might establish the truth of an analytic proposition, all three may in their different ways be taken as established. (There are, moreover, already very great differences between the different ways in which different sorts of facts may be established or attacked —but that is another story).

So let me now try and restate my position. First I should repeat that I should not at all wish to be taken as saying that truths are 'nothing but the confirmations of assertions',

---

[1] Though as I have tried to indicate in Chapter 11 in particular, this provision of 'speaking the same language' may by no means always be a straightforward one.

if this is to be understood as carrying the implicit suggestion that if there were no assertions to be confirmed, there would be neither facts nor reality nor, in short, anything at all. This is a position which I have already said that I regard as absurd. It was at this point that I felt, and still feel, most dubious about presenting an account of the meaning of 'true' which avowedly omits its frequent, if somewhat incoherent, reference to an independent reality. However, there is strictly speaking no question of the facts themselves being either true or false; these terms apply rather to particular accounts of how the facts are.[1] And although the facts, whatever they may be, are doubtless as they are, any particular account of how this is, is naturally open to challenge and hence to reaffirmation. It is the peculiar function of the word 'true' to confirm, affirm or reaffirm an assertion as one by which the speaker is unreservedly committed to stand. Fully committed (fully guaranteed) affirmations may be given on the relevant occasions to factual assertions of many different types, any justifications of which would have to proceed in as many different ways. But fully committed guarantees can also be given of assertions that are no type of factual statement at all. It follows that the justifications of such guarantees would have to proceed in even more different ways. They would still, however, be 'up to the hilt' guarantees. In this sense, the same sort of guarantees may be given for articles of very different sorts; and it is this which may justify us in using the one word 'true' throughout such a varied range of contextual circumstances.

However, if anyone still prefers to say that guarantees for such strikingly different sorts of assertions must ipso facto be counted as different sorts of guarantees, it need in the last resort hardly matter very much. What does matter is that we should see that analytic propositions, synthetic

[1] So speaking equally strictly, we should have to talk of 'reasons given in support of factual statements tending to establish the statement in question'.

propositions and value judgments are indeed different types of assertions; and, as I put it in the last sentence of Chapter 6, that "the different ways in which they may be confirmed or attacked are fundamental aspects of the ways in which they are all different from each other". (p. 91). For the rest, the question is essentially one of emphasis and terminology.

It goes without saying that there remain all sorts of philosophically important problems connected with the notion of 'truth' at which I have not even hinted here. In particular, there are the questions concerned with truth in formal systems and with the relation of these systems to all other philosophical problems. But here to end this discussion is just one final puzzling (and puzzled) consideration:—

This arises from the fact that in so far as one does accept the analogy between the uses of 'good' and 'true', one is naturally led to argue that just as the judgment that "X is good" must always be based upon reasons, so too must the judgment that a given story or assertion is true. And from this it is easy to assume that in the case of synthetic propositions, the reasons that must lie behind any judgment of truth or falsity must consist of the available evidence. Indeed, it is pretty clear that this is an assumption that I myself have made. There are, however, two considerations which tell very strongly against it. In the first place, as I have pointed out a few paragraphs ago, a man may sometimes maintain the truth of an assertion even in the face of the evidence or where it is in principle impossible to hope that any evidence may be forthcoming. Secondly, any supporting reasons for the judgment "X is good" must lie in certain factual characteristics of X; but this analogy will not work when it comes to questions of evidence for the truth of synthetic propositions. For the reasons which may relevantly be brought forward in support of a factual assertion do not usually lie within the actual characteristics of the assertion itself. There is nothing in the statement itself, for example, that could provide a justifying reason or evidence for the claim that it is true that there are black swans in Australia.

On the whole this seems to me to be yet another reason for restricting the use of such terms as 'value judgment', as I suggested on page 157, and for saying not that 'true' is a value-word, but that it is in some ways like one. I do still feel inclined to say that its meaning lies in the offer of a particular sort of 'up to the hilt' guarantee, and that the criteria on the basis of which such guarantees might be supported, vary according to the sort of assertion that is being guaranteed. But I have certainly shown that I remain in a muddle as to how exactly to elaborate this thesis. It is as well in the circumstances that this is not supposed to be a treatise on the concept of 'truth', and that I can fairly leave the consideration of this particular problem to another time.

BIBLIOGRAPHY

There are so many different directions in which someone who now wishes to read further in philosophy, might choose to go that it is not easy to know exactly what advice to offer. The following suggestions are inevitably somewhat arbitrary and by no means exhaust the possibilities.

A. Books.

(i). The three most considerable books on moral philosophy written from the modern analytical standpoint that have appeared in this country within the last few years are:—

The Place of Reason in Ethics, by S. E. Toulmin. (C.U.P., 1950).

The Language of Morals, by R. M. Hare. (O.U.P., 1952).

Ethics, by P. H. Nowell Smith. (Pelican, 1954).

In terms of subsequent controversy Hare's has probably been the most prominent of the three so far, while Nowell Smith's has the widest range; but they are all three contributions to one and the same discussion, and may best be read in comparison and contrast with each other. Another book of similar type, written in a most lively and readable manner, is *The Logic of Moral Discourse* by Paul Edwards, (The Free Press, Illinois, 1955); but this book appeared in America and has so far had on the whole less impact, in this country at any rate, than the other three. Two other books which may be helpful are Maurice Cranston's *Freedom—A New Analysis*, (Longmans, 1953), which is both short and admirably clear; and Austin Duncan Jones' *Butler's Moral Philosophy*, (Pelican, 1952), which combines an account of this eighteenth century philosopher with a running discussion, also very clear, of some of the central problems of moral philosophy.

(ii) These books, especially those by Toulmin, Hare and Nowell Smith, may, however, be somewhat easier to follow if the threads of the discussion are picked up a little further back in time. The shortest way of doing this would almost certainly be to go back to G. E. Moore's *Principia Ethica*, (C.U.P., 1903). In many ways this now strikes one as a quite extraordinarily wrong-headed book; but it has had, together with his later *Ethics*, (Home University Library, 1912), a very great influence on the subsequent course of moral philosophy in this country, not least as a mark to be shot at. A very fair sample of these subsequent shots (and of shots at other aspects of Moore's philosophy, which has been in general of at least equal importance and influence) may be found in *The Philosophy of G. E. Moore*, edited by P. A. Schilpp (North-western University, 1952), a collection of articles on Moore by a number of different philosophers, followed by his reply to his critics. Among these articles that by C. L. Stevenson is worth particular mention, especially for the indication it gives of the sort of line taken by Stevenson in his own important book *Ethics and Language*, (Yale University Press, 1944). Apart from this collection, A. N. Prior's excellent little book *Logic and the Basis of Ethics*, (O.U.P., 1949), provides a concise study in an historical perspective of one of the main themes of *Principia Ethica*. Finally in this exceedingly potted historical section, mention should be made of the chapter on ethics (Chapter 6) in A. J. Ayer's early logical positivist, anti-metaphysical work *Language, Truth and Logic*, (Gollancz, 1936—and 2nd edition, with an important new preface, 1946).

(iii). It is by no means obvious, however, that the best way to go on with the subject is to stick doggedly and exclusively to specifically moral philosophy, even if that is one's main interest; and some people may prefer as a next step to explore further the general philosophical background against which moral philosophy takes shape as an area of special enquiry. Here there is, of course, an even wider range of possibilities, and any suggested choice becomes correspondingly more invidious. However, a good and representative start at any rate could certainly be made with *Dilemmas* by Gilbert Ryle, (C.U.P., 1954), *The Problem of Knowledge* by A. J. Ayer (now very different in many ways from the Ayer of *Language, Truth and Logic*), (Pelican, 1956), and *Introduction to Logical Theory* by P. F. Strawson, (Methuen, 1952)—in order, I should say, of increasing difficulty. To this list may be added *The Concept of Mind*, also by Ryle, (Hutchinson, 1949), a varied discussion of a very varied selection of mental concepts; Ryle has already in fact modified or abandoned a fair number of the detailed arguments of this book, but it remains of first-rate importance as a focus of discussion in its field. Finally, for a short account of the general development of *English Philosophy since* 1900, G. J. Warnock's book of that title, (Home University Library, 1958), is brief, clear and wholly excelent; it also contains a useful little bibliography of its own.

B. Articles.

There are, of course, many other books that might well have been mentioned. In fact, however, by far the greater part of current work in philosophy is published rather in articles, and to follow the journals is much the best way of keeping in touch with current discussions. One way and another there are a surprisingly large number of philosophical journals published in English. In this country alone there are, among others, *Mind, The Philosophical Quarterly, Philosophy* and *Analysis*, all of which may contain articles on moral philosophy as well as on other topics. Of these, *Analysis* specialises in short discussion articles of a more or less technical nature, while *Philosophy* makes the greatest effort to appeal to a slightly wider audience than one of philosophers alone—though this in no way means that it sacrifices professional standards or interests. In addition, many important papers appear in the volumes published every year by the Aristotelian Society—(the Proceedings and their Supplementary Volumes). All these journals have in the last few years in particular seen a great burst of writing on problems of moral philosophy; and it would make for an excessively long list to mention all the relevant articles here. In any case, there is no better way of extending one's philosophical education than by browsing through old numbers of these journals, dipping in and out of articles and reviews to find out for oneself which ones are of interest.

Not everyone, of course, has easy access to the past numbers of such journals. Happily, however, there is already an imposing number of collections of the more important articles gathered together from the journals and reprinted in book form. Among the most useful of these articles on the whole range of problems of philosophical analysis are the two volumes of *Logic and Language*, (Blackwell, 1952 and 1953) and *Essays in Conceptual Analysis*, (Macmillan, 1956), all edited by A. G. N. Flew; while for those who wish to concentrate on moral philosophy as such, there is the large and excellent *Readings in Ethical Theory* edited by Wilfrid Sellars and John Hospers, (Appleton-Century-Crofts, 1952).

INDEX

Index

Index

Grant Ave
Office make appt mon